Pumkin Pie

From the kitchen of...

1½ Pumkin
1 Cup Sugar
1½ Cups Milk
3 eggs
1 teaspoon Cinnamon
½ nutmeg, a little Ginger

1 teaspoon Salt

OLD FARM

Country Cookbook

RECISES, MENUS, AND MEMORIES

JERRY APPS & SUSAN APPS-BODILLY

WISCONSIN HISTORICAL SOCIETY PRESS

Published by the Wisconsin Historical Society Press
Publishers since 1855

The Wisconsin Historical Society helps people connect to the past by collecting, preserving, and sharing stories. Founded in 1846, the Society is one of the nation's finest historical institutions.
Order books by phone toll free: 888-999-1669
Order books online: shop.wisconsinhistory.org
Join the Wisconsin Historical Society: wisconsinhistory.org/membership

Printed in Canada
Design and illustration by Steve Biel

26 25 24 23 22   3 4 5

Library of Congress Cataloging-in-Publication Data
Names: Apps, Jerold W., 1934– author. | Apps-Bodilly, Susan, author.
Title: Old farm country cookbook : recipes, menus, and memories / Jerry Apps
    and Susan Apps-Bodilly.
Description: Madison : Wisconsin Historical Society Press, [2017] | Includes
    bibliographical references and index.
Identifiers: LCCN 2016053381 (print) | LCCN 2017000093 (ebook) | ISBN
    9780870208300 (pbk. : alk. paper) | ISBN 9780870208317 ()
Subjects: LCSH: Cooking, American—Midwestern style. | Farm life—United
    States—History—20th century. | LCGFT: Cookbooks.
Classification: LCC TX715.2.M53 A676 2017 (print) | LCC TX715.2.M53 (ebook) |
    DDC 641.5977—dc23
LC record available at https://lccn.loc.gov/2016053381

To Eleanor Apps, who left behind a recipe box chock-full of wonderful things to cook and bake.

*A large group gathered around the Apps dining room table
for Thanksgiving dinner in the early 1960s.*

CONTENTS

ACKNOWLEDGMENTS

We wish to thank several people for making this book possible.

Eleanor Apps, Jerry's mother and Susan's grandmother, provided the inspiration, and her recipe box was the source for most of the recipes included here.

Ruth Apps, a professional home economist, helped test many of the recipes, looked over our work, and made many important suggestions for improving the manuscript.

The Wisconsin Historical Society Press, under the able leadership of Kathy Borkowski, deserves a big thank-you for its commitment to publishing works such as this.

And finally, Kate Thompson, senior editor at the Wisconsin Historical Society Press, whose idea it was to create this book, deserves enormous credit for her work in blending the stories and recipes to make something of lasting value.

Eleanor Apps as a young woman

INTRODUCTION

As I think back to the years when I was growing up on a small dairy farm in central Wisconsin during the latter years of the Great Depression and World War II, I don't know how my mother did it. Eleanor Apps did all of the baking and cooking for our family of five without electricity or running water, without a refrigerator, and using a wood-burning cookstove. And she did it well.

Those were challenging times. Farm income was meager during the 1930s, and during the war years that followed, rationing made Ma's work in the kitchen even more difficult. Yet her ever-present recipe box gave her the ideas and information she needed for providing wonderful meals. I don't remember ever going to bed hungry, although many children did during that time.

I remember so well when electricity came to our farm, in 1947, and a refrigerator replaced the icebox, a home freezer eliminated many jars of preserved food on the cellar shelves, and lightbulbs replaced kerosene lamps and lanterns. My mother added new recipes to her already long list, including such things as Jell-O and ice cream desserts that required refrigeration.

As I thought about those years, it occurred to me that people today might be interested in Ma's recipes and the role that food played in our lives in those days—for its importance went well beyond providing sustenance. Yet I know next to nothing about cooking. I do it on occasion, but I seem to have inherited my father's cooking skills, which my mother described with one phrase: "Your father can't boil water without burning it." I talked to my daughter, Susan, who is a teacher, an author, and a good cook, and she agreed to co-write this book with me, taking charge of the menus, recipes, and illustrations. My wife, Ruth, a professional home economist, agreed to "help out as needed." She read everything Sue and I wrote, tested many of the recipes, and checked all of them to make sure they were accurate. She was of great help in providing directions that were often missing on my mother's recipe cards.

In the days of my youth, preparing food from scratch was the way things were done, and people knew what was in their food and where it came from. Good food was at the center of our family and social affairs, especially those times when neighbors got together to help each other at threshing, sawing, silo-filling, and corn-shredding bees. For me, food will always be associated with those times of good eating, storytelling, laughter, and good-hearted fun.

—Jerry Apps

My grandma Eleanor Apps's white wooden box, with a hinged lid that flips up, holds recipe cards. They are simple lined index cards, scraps of paper, or little pieces of cardboard. On the cards are recipes for cakes and cookies, salads and breads, written with blue ink in her cursive handwriting.

A closer look reveals a story. It's a story of many hours of work, of time spent preparing meals for her family and others who ate at the kitchen

or dining room tables. The cards are yellowed and covered with food spills, and often in the top right corner is the name of a sister, a friend, or a neighbor who shared something of themselves by sharing a recipe.

These cards are written in the language of food from that time: *a pinch of this, season with salt and pepper to taste, bake for about an hour.* Why is there no mention of an oven temperature? My grandma cooked on a woodstove and knew the kind and amount of wood to use to heat the oven for baking pies, a hotdish, or bread. Why is there no mention of a mixer or blender? Her early kitchen did not have electricity; she mixed, chopped, and stirred by hand.

Susie licking the beaters—her first "recipe" experience—in 1965

When I was young, I visited my grandparents' farm often and stayed for a week in the summer to help during strawberry-picking season. By that time the kitchen had electricity and indoor plumbing. I remember Grandma's homemade sweet rolls and doughnuts and the smell of date cookies in the oven. At breakfast we ate fried eggs with lots of pepper and piles of buttered toast. Her salads had fresh-picked peas and lettuce with chunks of ham and cheddar cheese. She showed me how to gather eggs out of the nests in the chicken house and insisted I watch her pluck feathers from a recently butchered chicken to prepare it for roasting. I never actually saw my grandma cook with a recipe card. Most of her cards have no directions at all, just lists of ingredients. I imagine she simply knew how to cook and used the cards to jog her memory.

Why would I attempt to cook the way she did when my father and his twin brothers were young? When I follow her recipes, I remember her; I connect with her way of life in the kitchen. For this cookbook, I rewrote her recipes for cooks in today's kitchen, adding oven temperatures and pan sizes and clarifying, where I could, the language of the era. However, I put away my mixer and fancy gadgets and picked up my wooden spoons and potato masher. My mother and I got out our canning supplies to make grape and raspberry jam.

I have cooked or baked most of the recipes in this book. (I decided not to fry up a squirrel!) I did so to honor my grandma and all the women who worked in the kitchen for their families. Some folks say it was a simpler time. I don't think so! I think these women worked very hard and were very smart to plan, prepare, and cook meals for their family and at times for large groups of men who helped the farm at harvesting time.

I use these recipe cards, I listen to my father's stories, and I remember my grandma. I think about how these recipes connected them to their own heritage and how food connected a family as they sat around the kitchen table for breakfast after chores. I think about how they used food to celebrate a birthday, mourn the passing of a family member, greet a new neighbor, or have fun on a holiday.

Why do I care about a pile of old, yellowed, food-stained cards? When I use Grandma Apps's recipes, she is with me in the kitchen. She is still here. I remember her through this white wooden box of recipes.

—*Susan Apps-Bodilly*

PART ONE

KITCHEN MEMORIES

CHAPTER 1

THE HEART OF THE HOME

The farmhouse I grew up in was built around 1900. It had a large kitchen, smaller dining room and parlor, and five bedrooms, two of them downstairs and three upstairs. We heated the house with two woodstoves: a cookstove in the kitchen and a larger stove in the dining room. As was common for rural houses at the time, the house was not insulated and had no storm windows. On winter mornings it was as cold inside the house as it was outside—or so it seemed to me.

The home of Eleanor and Herman Apps

The kitchen was the center of all activity on the farm. It was there that the food was prepared and consumed. There we entertained visitors, unless it was warm enough to be outside (the exception was city relatives, whom Ma seated in the little-used parlor). There farming plans were made and shared, Sears and Roebuck orders written, garden seed orders prepared, and baby pigs and chicks warmed on cold spring nights. The smell of our kitchen was a mixture of fermenting sauerkraut, wood smoke, baking bread, and the barn smells brought in with the barn clothes. It was a warm and cozy place, especially in the depths of winter. It could also get mighty warm on a hot July day, especially if Ma was baking bread, which she did at least twice a week.

A big wooden table stood in the center of the room, with five well-worn wooden chairs pushed up to it. Our family of five ate all of our meals sitting around the kitchen table, each in our place: Pa at one end, Ma at the other, me on one side, and my twin brothers facing me on the other. In this way we were like the cows in our barn; each cow had its own stall, without variation.

A red-and-white-checked oilcloth covered the table, and in the middle of it was a kerosene lamp, the kitchen's main source of illumination. The wood-burning cookstove stood a few feet away from the west kitchen wall, its black stovepipe thrusting out from its back and connecting to a brick

Eleanor's first wood-burning cookstove was similar to this one.

chimney. Black with a bit of silver-colored trim, the stove had four lids on its flat top, a warming oven a foot or so above the top, a reservoir on the right side that kept water warm when the stove was in operation, and an

CAST-IRON SKILLET

A twelve-inch cast-iron skillet was my mother's main cooking utensil. She used it for nearly everything, from frying bacon, eggs, and potatoes for breakfast, to frying fresh-caught bluegills, pork chops, ham, and even fried sauerkraut—yes, we ate sauerkraut fried in bacon grease. And that's not to mention the squirrels, rabbits, and venison that found their way into Ma's skillet. On winter days when the temperature dipped below zero, Ma used the skillet to make pancakes, a welcome sight when we came in after finishing our barn chores.

When it wasn't in use, the cast-iron skillet was stored inside the oven, so it would always be at the ready. I don't recall Ma ever buying a new one, and I imagine hers was a wedding present—what better gift for a farm bride?

BUCKWHEAT PANCAKES

1 egg
1 cup milk
2 tablespoons shortening, melted
½ cup buckwheat flour
½ cup wheat flour
1 tablespoon sugar
2 teaspoons baking powder
½ teaspoon salt

Beat the egg in a bowl. Stir in all the other ingredients until smooth. Do not overmix.

Grease a skillet and set on medium heat. Sprinkle a few drops of water on the skillet to see if it is hot enough; if the drops sizzle around, the skillet is ready. Pour a spoonful of batter into the skillet. Cook the pancake until bubbles begin to form. Flip the pancake over to cook on the other side. Cook until golden brown.

oven underneath with a big door that pulled open to allow access. A large teakettle sat on the stove at all times, providing hot water for cooking, warming up water for Saturday night baths, and making whiskey slings when one of us got a cold. (Recipe for a whiskey sling: Pour a jigger of whiskey into a glass of warm water, then add a little lemon or honey to help the concoction go down.)

A sink stood on the north wall of the kitchen, with a little counter space on each side. To the left of the sink was a water pail with a dipper hanging at its side. If you wanted a drink of water, you slipped the dipper into the pail and scooped out what you wanted—making sure to drink all of it, as water was not to be wasted. That single pail of water was the source for my mother's cooking, for washing hands and brushing teeth, and for filling the ever-present teakettle. When the pail was empty, one of my brothers or I carried it to the pump house, lifted the handle to engage the windmill, and refilled the pail.

The icebox stood to the right of the sink, and next to the icebox was the door to the pantry, where such things as flour, sugar, and other staples were stored. A big crock of sauerkraut stood in the pantry from late autumn throughout the winter—or until all the kraut was consumed. On the far end of the pantry was the door to the stairway leading to the cellar, where all of home-canned goods could be found: fruits, vegetables, and meats in glass jars all stacked neatly on rows of wooden shelves that Pa had built. A smoked ham and a smoked side of bacon hung on hooks along the cellar stairway.

In winter, the only entrance to our farmhouse was via the kitchen. Ma didn't want visitors traipsing through the dining room on their way to the kitchen, which is where you'd find her working at the kitchen stove most of the time in winter. Besides, closing the dining room door for the winter prevented cold air from entering the house in one more place. Doing so was common practice, and farm people knew the kitchen door was the entryway into a house. In fact, my folks pushed a bureau against our formal front door, which led to the dining room, so it was impossible to open. A city person—usually a salesman of some stripe—could be quickly identified as such if he tried to enter the house through the front door.

Off the kitchen was the dining room, a tad smaller. A door on the south wall of the dining room led to Ma and Pa's bedroom; the front door of the

THE WATKINS MAN

The Watkins man visited our farm once a month, sometimes twice. He was one of many traveling salesmen who came by the farm trying to sell us everything from commercial cattle feed to magazine subscriptions. The Watkins man was special, mainly because Ma allowed him to come into the house, and she occasionally bought something from him.

My brothers and I were intrigued by the Watkins man and the big leather display case he carried into the house. I think Ma enjoyed his visits as well, especially in the winter, when opportunities to talk with folks outside the family were limited. He remembered our names, too, often beginning his spiel with "Well, Eleanor, what can I help you with today?"

As he talked he removed items from his black leather bag, lining them up on the table. Watkins salve in a big tin: "Cure just about any sore or scratch that comes along." Watkins liniment in a big bottle: "Good for horses, good for chickens, good for cows, and by golly, good for people, too." He kept removing items from the bottomless black bag until the kitchen table looked like the Watkins display at the county fair.

My brothers and I stood watching and listening and wondering if Ma would buy anything this time. I suspect the Watkins man was wondering the same thing as he continued talking about the virtues of each item. "Nobody has better vanilla than Watkins"; "Gotta go some to beat Watkins pepper."

On occasion, Ma bought vanilla, allspice, cinnamon, or pepper from the Watkins man, and that was enough to keep him coming back. Pa also regularly bought Watkins liniment and Watkins salve, maybe twice a year depending on the health of the farm animals—and the health of the family.

house, on the east end of the room, led outside; a pair of double doors opened to the parlor; and yet another door led to the stairway leading upstairs. From late October until the following April, a wood-burning stove, Round Oak brand, stood a few feet from the dining room's south wall, with its stovepipe thrust through the ceiling where it entered the chimney in the room above—the bedroom where my brothers and I slept during the cold months of the year. The stove had a big door on one side, large enough so an unsplit block of wood would fit inside. It had a smaller door beneath the larger one, where the ashes could be removed—an everyday task when the stove was burning. (An ash pile accumulated on the north side of the house throughout the fall and winter and was hauled and spread on our vegetable garden each spring—wood ashes make good fertilizer.) The stove was black with silver trim, and it stood on four legs that lifted it about a foot above the floor.

From October to April, the front door was blocked off, and the double doors to the parlor were opened only when we needed to retrieve an item of clothing from the small, unused bedroom off the parlor. The parlor was used only for special occasions, such as visits from city relatives or a meeting of the church's Ladies Aid group.

After the kitchen, the dining room was the most used room in the house. In the center stood a six-foot wooden table; with leaves added it could seat a crew of neighbors working on threshing, corn husking, silo filling, or wood sawing—as many as fourteen or sixteen hungry men.

In addition to accommodating the work crews, the dining room table was the center of our Thanksgiving and Christmas celebrations, when the aunts, uncles, and cousins joined us. And it was around the extended dining room table that the quilters gathered to sew quilts on cold and dreary winter afternoons.

A party-line telephone that operated with batteries was fastened to the wall near the front door, adjacent to three large windows that lit the dining room during daylight hours. The phone, wooden with a talking piece jutting out from its front, a listening device hanging on the left side, and a crank on the right side for ringing, was answered only by our mother. Our number was 168 and our ring was a long and three shorts, but Ma usually "listened in" to other conversations when the ring wasn't ours, a common way in those days of keeping up with what was going on in the neighborhood.

On the east wall, a loud-ticking windup clock stood on a clock shelf, a reminder to me when I got up in the morning that I was probably going to be late arriving in the barn for milking. Pa expected me in the barn by quarter of six each morning, every day of the year. On cold winter mornings, I dressed by the Round Oak heating stove, which Pa had started before leaving for the barn. The trip from my frigid bedroom and down an even more frigid hall and stairway had chilled me to the bone, and I tried to warm myself as I dressed. The clock's "tick-tock, tick-tock" was a steady reminder to quickly pull on my clothes, grab my barn lantern, and hurry through the sharply cold morning to the warm barn.

In addition to the clock, the shelf held any important correspondence. Under the shelf sat a couch where we rested when we didn't feel well and where Pa rested after a hard day's work.

My family didn't spend much time in the dining room during the summer months; there was just too much to do on the farm. In late March, Pa enlisted a couple of neighbors to help him haul the heavy woodstove out to the wood-shed, where it sat until fall. We knew winter was on the way when the men hauled the old woodstove back into the dining room, positioned the stovepipes, brushed off the dust and dirt accumulated over the summer, and started the fire to make sure everything was properly in place.

I have fond memories of winter evenings when the snow was piled high and the temperature was below zero as the five of us sat around the dining room table. The Round Oak stove filled with blocks of oak wood kept the room cozy warm. A kerosene lamp sat in the middle of the table, casting enough light so my brothers and I could do our homework, Ma could work on her mending—darning socks and patching bib overalls and the elbows of flannel shirts—and Pa could read the *Milwaukee Sentinel* and the *Wisconsin Agriculturist*.

One cold winter afternoon when I was about three years old, my uncle George was looking after me while the folks had gone to town. I had just gotten Tinker Toys for Christmas, and Uncle George and I spent that afternoon at the dining room table making the most wonderful creations. Tinker Toys consisted of wooden spools with holes drilled in them, plus wooden sticks that could be placed in the holes. We made a barn and a shed and a windmill that actually worked. We laughed when our creations didn't work— which was often. During a break from our building projects, we ate my mother's molasses cookies, with coffee for Uncle George and milk for me. Uncle George was a quiet man, a bachelor who lived with my grandfather in Wild Rose. On this winter afternoon, I had him all to myself, and we got to know each other around that old wooden table.

Eleanor's Molasses Cookies

2 cups sugar

1 cup shortening

4 eggs, divided

1 cup molasses

4 cups flour, plus ½ cup flour to use while rolling out

2 teaspoons baking soda

2 teaspoons cinnamon

½ teaspoon cloves

½ teaspoon ginger

½ teaspoon salt

Blend the sugar and shortening until fluffy. Add 3 of the eggs and the molasses. Mix well. In another bowl, mix the 4 cups flour with the baking soda, cinnamon, cloves, ginger, and salt. Add the flour mixture gradually to the egg mixture to make dough. Refrigerate for 2 hours or overnight.

Preheat oven to 350 degrees and lightly grease a cookie sheet. Roll out about one-third of the dough on a floured pastry cloth to about ¼-inch thick. Keep the rest cold until ready to roll out. Cut out the cookies with a favorite cookie cutter and place on the cookie sheet. Beat the remaining egg with a fork. Brush a bit of the beaten egg on each cookie. Bake until just set, about 10 minutes. Cool on a wire rack. Continue making cookies with remaining dough.

CHAPTER 2

WOODSTOVE COOKING

"Jerold, the woodbox is empty."

Hearing this call from my mother is one of my earliest memories, for beginning when I was about three years old, one of my chores was to keep the woodbox near the kitchen stove filled, in all months of the year. When I had other, more important things to do, such as playing with the little barn and toy animals I'd gotten for Christmas or paging through the Uncle Wiggily book that my mother read to me at bedtime, she often called for more wood.

A woodshed, an extension on the west side of the kitchen, held the stovewood that Pa had split and stacked. It was mostly dried oak, with a little pinewood that Pa called kindlin'. The oak he had cut from the woodlot north of our farmhouse, the pine from a dead tree in the windbreak west of the buildings. Filling the woodbox was not an especially difficult task. I merely had to trot through the kitchen, open the door to the woodshed, gather up an armful of wood, return to the kitchen, and dump it in the woodbox standing to the left of the cookstove.

"Be careful you don't make a mess," Ma would say, meaning she didn't want me to drop a stick of wood on the kitchen floor and stir up a bunch of dust.

Every day of the year, Pa started the cookstove before going out to the barn for the morning milking. Ma kept the stove going all day, until we all went to bed around nine every evening. I kept the woodbox filled until my brothers were old enough to take over the task and I moved to higher-level chores, such as helping with the milking and other barn chores.

Ma used the cookstove to do all the cooking, baking, and canning, plus heating water for washday and our Saturday night baths. The oven did not have a thermometer, but Ma knew just by opening the door and holding her hand inside for a moment if the oven was at the proper temperature for whatever she was baking. She adjusted the temperature by the type and amount of wood she put in the stove's firebox. (Oak wood gives off more heat and holds it longer than pine wood, for instance.) To know if the top of the stove was hot enough to fry eggs or potatoes, she would drop a little cold water on the stove's lid; if the water sizzled and bounced, it was hot enough. Cooking and baking with a wood-burning cookstove was an art, one my mother mastered.

I have wonderful memories of not just the comforting heat that came from our old stove but also the aromas of baking bread, ham cooking with sauerkraut, and thick-sliced bacon sizzling on a cold winter morning. Ma baked

WOOD FOR WOODSTOVE COOKING

For those who have access to a woodlot, the best kind of wood is that which is readily available. But different types of wood have different qualities, and the best wood for woodstove cooking, in order of heating value, are hickory, white oak, black oak, birch, and black locust.

Soft white and red pine, especially when cut into small, thin pieces for kindling, are good for starting a fire because they burn fast. Harder woods, especially the oaks, are better choices for cooking because they burn more slowly.

Although I have plenty of black locust available on my farm, I generally avoid burning it because of the smell of its smoke. Locust is a legume, and when it burns it gives off a rather foul odor. I prefer the sweet smell of oak, hickory, and birch smoke.

I also cure the wood for at least a year before burning it. Freshly cut wood can contain up to 50 percent moisture. After several months of curing (sitting covered in a dry spot), the wood's moisture level drops to 25 percent or lower. Some moisture in wood is a good thing, though; if wood is allowed to dry for several years, it tends to burn too quickly and won't maintain the heat necessary for woodstove cooking.

a half dozen loaves of bread a week. (We never purchased bread from the store. Pa said bakers' bread, as he called it, "had no power in it.")

Ma's strawberry sweet rolls, with homemade strawberry jam baked into them, were special Sunday morning treats. And about once a month, more often in winter, Ma fried up a batch of doughnuts in a big kettle of oil, including the little round doughnut holes, all of them coated with sugar and prized by my brothers and me.

WOODSTOVE POPCORN

Every so often on a cold winter night, Ma would announce that it was a good night for popcorn. As the snow fell and the wind howled, sometimes sending a little puff of wood smoke into the kitchen, we stoked up the fire so it would be good and hot, which made popping corn quite easy.

Ma took out one of her big cooking pots, one with a handle and a cover. She cut a slice of butter into the pot and put it on the stove. When the butter was melted, she dropped in a small handful of popcorn. We'd take turns jiggling the pot back and forth on the hot stove, waiting for the first kernel to pop and then the explosion of kernels all popping at once with the wonderful smell of popped corn and melted butter oozing from under the cover of the cook pot and filling the kitchen. When the popping lessened, someone (usually Ma) had to decide when it was time to remove the pot from the stove. Leave the pot on the stove too long and you risked burning some of the popcorn; take it off too soon and you might have a cluster of "old maids," or unpopped corn. After removing the pot from the stove, Ma dumped the freshly popped corn into a big bowl, sprinkled on a little salt, and we dove in. What a wonderful treat it was.

Basic Sweet Dough

8–9 cups all-purpose flour, divided
1 cup sugar
1 teaspoon salt
3 packages (¼ ounce each) active dry yeast (can also make this
    using cake yeast; see note below)
1½ cups milk
½ cup water
1 cup butter
2 eggs

In a large bowl, combine 2 cups of the flour, sugar, salt, and yeast.

Heat milk, water, and butter in a medium saucepan over low heat until very warm—about 120–130 degrees.

Slowly pour milk mixture into flour mixture. Mix until blended, scraping the sides of the bowl. Stir in about 4⅓ cups of the remaining flour, enough to make a smooth, soft dough. Turn the dough onto a lightly floured surface and knead until smooth and elastic, 8 to 10 minutes. Shape the dough into a ball and place in a large greased bowl. Turn the dough greased side up. Cover with a towel and place the bowl in a warm place. Let rest until the dough is doubled in size, 1 to 1½ hours. The dough is ready if an indentation remains when the dough is touched.

Punch down the dough. Turn dough onto lightly floured surface.

TO MAKE BASIC SWEET DOUGH USING CAKE YEAST:
Use one 2-ounce cake of yeast and decrease the total liquid in the recipe by ½ cup to adjust for the liquid used to dissolve the yeast. Dissolve 1 teaspoon sugar in ½ cup milk heated to 90–95 degrees. Add crumbled cake yeast to sugar solution. Stir until completely dissolved. Let mixture sit 5 to 10 minutes until the yeast begins to bubble. Add yeast mixture to the remaining ingredients.

Cinnamon Rolls

1 cup brown sugar
2 teaspoons cinnamon
Basic Sweet Dough (recipe on previous page)
½ cup butter, melted

Mix the brown sugar and cinnamon.

Roll half of Basic Sweet Dough into a 12 x 18-inch rectangle. Spread with half of the butter and sprinkle with half of the brown sugar and cinnamon mixture. Starting at the long (18-inch) side, roll up dough tightly. Pinch the edge of the dough into the roll to seal well. Repeat with the other half of the dough and remaining filling.

Use kitchen string to cut the dough into 1- to 1½-inch-thick slices: slide the string under the roll and pull it up toward you, crossing the strings, to "cut" the dough. Grease a 9-inch square or 8-inch round pan. Place rolls slightly apart in pan. Cover with a towel and set in a warm place. Let rise until doubled in size, about 40 minutes.

Preheat oven to 400 degrees. Bake until golden brown, 25 to 30 minutes.

Fried Doughnuts

1 cup sugar
1 tablespoon butter
1 egg
3 egg yolks
½ cup milk
½ cup cream
½ teaspoon nutmeg
4 cups flour
5 teaspoons baking powder
1 teaspoon salt
½ teaspoon baking soda
Vegetable oil for frying
Powdered sugar for dusting

Cream sugar and butter together in a large bowl. Beat in egg, then beat in the egg yolks one at a time. Stir in the milk gradually, then the cream and the nutmeg. In a separate bowl, mix flour, baking powder, salt, and baking soda. Stir dry mixture into the sugar mixture, blending well.

Fill a large pan with vegetable oil to 2 to 3 inches deep. Heat to 375 degrees.

Roll the dough onto lightly floured pastry cloth, rolling it around to coat it with flour. Roll out gently to ⅜-inch thick with a rolling pin. Cut out the doughnuts with a floured doughnut cutter. Lift them out of the rolled dough with a wide spatula to keep the shape. Slide the doughnuts into hot oil and fry until golden brown, 2 to 3 minutes. (The doughnut holes are fried up the same as the doughnuts. They fry up round.) Turn doughnuts as soon as they rise to the surface. Drain on a paper-towel-lined tray. Dust with powdered sugar.

White Bread

2 cups milk
2 tablespoons sugar
1 tablespoon lard or shortening
2 teaspoons salt
1 package (¼ ounce) active dry yeast
¼ cup warm water (110 to 115 degrees)
6–7 cups flour, divided
Melted butter for tops of loaves

Scald the milk (heat it to 82 degrees) until small bubbles begin to form around the edges. Stir in the sugar, lard, and salt. Put in a large bowl and let cool to lukewarm.

In another bowl, sprinkle yeast over warm water and stir to mix and dissolve. When the yeast is dissolved, add it to the milk mixture. Add 3 cups of the flour and mix with a wooden spoon until the batter is smooth.

Add remaining flour, a little at a time, until you have a dough that holds together and pulls away from the sides of the bowl. Turn the dough onto a lightly floured board. Cover with a cloth and let rest for 10 minutes.

Knead the dough with floured hands until it is smooth and elastic, 8 to 10 minutes. To knead, fold the dough toward you and then push it away with the heels of your hands in a rocking motion. Turn the dough a quarter turn. Repeat the pushing motion with both of your hands. Round up the ball of dough and put it into a lightly greased bowl. Then turn the dough over so there is grease on the top. Cover and let the dough rise in a warm place until it is doubled in size, about 1 to 1½ hours.

Punch the dough down: push your fist into the center of the dough ball, releasing air bubbles from the dough. Cover the dough and let rise again until almost doubled in size, about 45 minutes.

Turn the dough onto the floured board and shape into a ball. Divide the dough in half, shape into 2 loaves, and place in 2 greased loaf pans. Cover and let rise in the pans until doubled in size, about 1 hour.

Preheat oven to 400 degrees. Bake bread until deep, golden brown, about 35 minutes. Brush tops with melted butter. Remove pans from oven and place on wire racks to cool.

CHAPTER 3

THE ICEBOX

Against the north wall of our kitchen, next to the sink, stood the icebox. It was creamy white, scarred and scratched from years of use. But it was dependable. It had no moving parts and was simply an insulated piece of kitchen furniture with two purposes: to keep things cool in summer and, somewhat ironically, to keep things from freezing on cold winter nights.

A metal drainpipe thrust out from the bottom of the icebox and into a hole that Pa had drilled through the kitchen floor. The water from the melting ice drained to a mysterious area under the kitchen (the house's cellar didn't reach this far).

The icebox stood about five feet tall and had a door on the top that opened to a compartment where the ice was kept. A door in the front allowed access to a couple of shelves, where Ma kept the butter, milk, and other foods she didn't want to spoil during the hot days of summer.

The iceman, a huge, burly man as I remember him, drove a truck filled with fifty-pound cakes of ice, which were covered with sawdust to keep them from melting. He wore a long canvas apron that covered him from just under his chin to below his knees. He came to our farm once a week in summer, backed his truck up to the kitchen porch, and knocked on the kitchen door. He was a friendly chap, always ready with a word about the weather or something he had seen on his trip from the icehouse on the shores of the Wild Rose Millpond to his bevy of customers scattered throughout the area.

"Got any ice left?" was his usual question.

"A little," Ma usually answered. How much depended on how hot the previous week had been. The iceman removed the remnants of the ice he had delivered the week before—sometimes mere scrapings, sometimes a sizable hunk. He deposited the leftover ice in the kitchen sink, walked back to his truck, lifted the canvas covering, and with ice tongs pulled out a fifty-pound cake of ice. With a little broom, he whisked away the sawdust,

HARVESTING ICE

Before electrical power came to homes and farms, ice was harvested from lakes and millponds and was delivered by the icemen who traveled the area filling iceboxes each week. The Wild Rose Millpond was our source for ice, and it was an excellent one, for the millpond had been formed by damming the clean and clear Pine River. An icehouse stood on the shore of the millpond, not far from the gristmill, and a second one was located on the other end of the millpond, just off Main Street.

The ice harvest usually began in late January or early February, after the ice had formed to a depth of twenty-four inches or more. The ideal air temperature for ice harvesting was about ten to fifteen degrees. The ice was cleared of snow with a team and a scraper, and then a team pulling a marker etched a half-inch groove in the ice, forming a checkerboard pattern of ice blocks to be cut. Men chopped a hole in the ice at the end of one of the etched lines and then sawed down the line using an ice saw (which looked like a logging saw but longer, about forty inches). Soon blocks of ice were floating in the cold water. The men lifted them out with ice tongs, a device with two hand-holds and sharp grippers that dug into ice. The blocks of freshly cut ice were then loaded onto a sled pulled by a team to an icehouse, where they were stacked with ample amounts of sawdust between them for insulation.

Every day during the warm months, the delivery man would stop at one of the icehouses, load his truck with blocks of ice, and make the rounds of the community. If a family wasn't home, they left a sign in the window indicating how much ice they wanted: fifty pounds, twenty-five pounds, or no ice that day. No one locked their houses in those days, so the iceman would come in, deposit the hunk of ice, and be on his way.

and then, using the tongs and one hand, he carried the heavy hunk of slippery, dripping ice into the kitchen and eased it into the icebox's top compartment. A trail of small puddles followed him.

If the leftover piece of ice was large enough, my brothers and I would appeal to Ma for some homemade ice cream. The entire family had long declared homemade ice cream far superior to the store-bought kind, which we nevertheless occasionally purchased with our nickel allowances on Saturday nights in town.

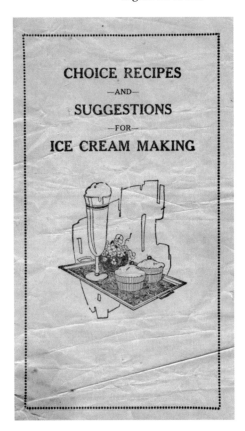

We rustled up the ice-cream maker from its storage place in the woodshed. It was the kind with a wooden tub into which a metal container was immersed and fastened to a hand-crank. We chipped the ice into little pieces with an ice pick, filling the wooden tub with the chips, and covered each layer with table salt to slow the melting. Ma poured the cooled ice cream mixture into the metal container.

My brothers and I took turns cranking until the crank became difficult to turn, a sign that the ice cream was ready. We removed the container, pulled out the wooden paddles covered in freshly frozen ice cream, and argued about who got to "lick the paddles."

Soon we were enjoying bowls of homemade ice cream, topped with whatever berries were in season. It truly was tastier than any store-bought ice cream.

Homemade Ice Cream

2 cups milk
¾ cup sugar
Pinch of salt
1 cup half-and-half
1 cup heavy cream
1½ teaspoons vanilla extract
½ cup mix-ins: chocolate chips, chopped nuts, or fruit (optional)

Scald the milk in a large pan or pot until bubbles form at the edge. Remove from heat. Add the sugar and salt and stir until they are dissolved. Stir in the half-and-half, heavy cream, and vanilla. Refrigerate the mixture at this point for 30 minutes to 1 hour until it is well chilled.

Start the ice-cream maker and pour mixture through the hole in the lid. Churn until ice cream is desired consistency, 20 to 40 minutes. If adding optional mix-ins, do so after the mixture begins to get thick and has started to freeze. Follow the freezing directions for your ice-cream maker. Makes about 2 quarts of ice cream.

TIPS FOR MAKING ICE CREAM WITH A HAND-CRANK ICE-CREAM MAKER:

1. Use the freshest ingredients available, especially fruits.

2. Have crushed ice and rock salt at the ready. The ideal proportion of ice to salt in your ice-cream maker is three to one.

3. Never fill the inside container, or can, of an ice-cream maker more than three-quarters full. If it gets too full, the ice cream can become grainy.

4. After pouring the ice-cream mixture into the can, nestle the can into a tub. Gradually alternate layers of ice and salt around the can and let it settle in. Finish with rock salt at the top.

(Continued next page)

(Continued from page 27)

5. Let everything sit for 5 minutes to chill before beginning to turn the crank.

6. While you are cranking your ice-cream mixture, add ice around the can as it melts away and layer with more rock salt. Don't take any water out.

7. Continue turning the crank until the ice cream is solid, about 20 minutes.

8. Wipe the top of the can clean of ice and salt water before looking in to check it.

9. Some say that, if you can wait, the ice cream tastes better after it "ripens." Remove the dasher and pack the ice cream down with a long wooden spoon. Put the cover back on tightly and place a cork in the hole where the dasher was. Put the can back in the tub; pack it with three parts ice and one part salt. Cover the ice cream with a thick covering or blanket and let it sit in the shade for two hours.

Icebox Cookies

1 cup white sugar
1 cup brown sugar
1 cup shortening
3 eggs, beaten
1 tablespoon vanilla
5 cups flour
2 teaspoons baking soda
1 teaspoon salt
Salted nuts or raisins (optional)

Cream sugars and shortening in a large bowl. Add the beaten eggs and vanilla. Set aside. In another bowl, mix the flour, baking soda, and salt. Add the flour mixture gradually to the sugar mixture and stir until blended into dough. Add nuts or raisins, or both, if desired. Divide dough into 4 portions and shape into rolls on a floured board with your hands. The rolls should be about 2 inches in diameter. Wrap in wax paper and refrigerate overnight.

Preheat oven to 375 degrees. Remove dough rolls from the refrigerator and slice them about ¼-inch thick. Bake on ungreased cookie sheets until lightly browned, 8 to 10 minutes.

Cranberry Jell-O Salad

1 package (3 ounces) raspberry Jell-O
1 package (3 ounces) lemon Jell-O
3 cups hot water
2 cups ground fresh cranberries
1 small orange, peeled and diced
1 small apple, peeled and diced
1 cup crushed pineapple with its liquid
1½ cups sugar
1 cup finely chopped celery
¼ cup chopped nuts

Mix both packages of Jell-O together in a large bowl. Pour hot water over the Jell-O and stir to dissolve. Add all the other ingredients. Pour into a serving bowl or mold and chill until set.

WHEN ELECTRICITY ARRIVED

Not long after the Rural Electrification Act of 1935 was passed, in the depths of the Depression, electricity began arriving in rural communities. By 1944, our country school had electricity, which meant that now an electric motor pumped water and lightbulbs replaced the gas lanterns. But the school board never saw fit to put in central heating or indoor plumbing, so the woodstove and the outhouses remained.

By the time the Rural Electrification Administration (REA) began setting poles and running wires to farms in Waushara County, where we lived, World War II had begun, copper wire was in short supply, and labor had changed its focus to the war effort. The farmers in our neighborhood made do with kerosene lamps and lanterns all through the war. When the war ended in summer 1945, the REA once more began signing up and lighting up farmsteads, but we were not "hooked up" until the spring of 1947.

Preserving meat had always been a challenge; smoking worked well, and storing pork chops in lard preserved them, but fresh meat was what many of us missed. Locker plants, usually associated with a meat market, began appearing during the war, offering a place where those of us without electricity could freeze and store meat. Pa rented a frozen food locker at a meat market in Almond, a village about nine miles from our farm. So for a few years we enjoyed fresh, frozen meat, but we had to drive nine miles to get it.

In the fall of 1946, electricians wired our house and the outbuildings after Pa had negotiated with the electric company to bring electricity to our farm. But the ground froze that fall before the poles from the main line could be set, and we waited until the following spring for everything to be in place. When my brothers and I returned home from school one day in April, Pa had a big smile on his face—for the first time ever we had electric power on our farm.

The bright lights took some getting used to after years of quiet yellow light from lamps and lanterns, but no one complained. Pa wasted little time before purchasing an electric motor for our water pump, an electric motor-driven milking machine, and a refrigerator for Ma's kitchen. We moved the icebox out to the woodshed and placed the shiny new refrigerator where the icebox had stood. Now we would have cold milk in

ABOVE IS THE JELL-O PACKAGE

ANYTHING SOLD IN ANY OTHER KIND OF PACKAGE IS NOT JELL-O. DON'T ASK FOR A "JELLY POWDER" WHEN YOU WANT JELL-O, BUT ASK FOR JELL-O, AND LOOK AT THE PACKAGE.

THE FAMOUS JELL-O DESSERTS CANNOT BE MADE WITH ANYTHING BUT JELL-O.

ALMOND-CHERRY JELL-O
RECIPE ON PAGE 11.

summer (the icebox at best kept things cool but never cold). And Ma could finally make Jell-O in summer, which required cooling to set. In those days, when some farmers had electricity and some did not, you could tell who did by observing who brought Jell-O dishes to summer gatherings.

Pa also bought a chest freezer, and he closed out the frozen food locker we'd been renting in Almond. Food preservation changed dramatically at the Apps home. We still enjoyed smoked bacon and ham, but pork chops, pork roasts, and other pork cuts were now frozen and stored in the freezer. Rather than canning green beans, peas, sweet corn, strawberries, blueberries, and raspberries, Ma froze them. She continued to can applesauce and make jams and jellies that she stored in jars, and sauerkraut preparation remained the same.

Without a doubt, electricity had transformed our lives in ways we could scarcely understand at the time. Now we on the farm had most of the same conveniences that our city relatives had. Ma could quit worrying about what city relatives thought when they visited and had to eat by the light of a kerosene lamp. But because we had an ample supply of free firewood, the wood-burning cookstove remained, as did the daily tasks of carrying in water, for indoor plumbing was still many years away.

CHAPTER 4

EARLY TO RISE

As was common for farm people, breakfast was a big meal at the Apps home. We got up at five thirty—even earlier in summer—to do the morning milking and barn chores, and by the time we came back into the house around seven, we were hungry. The breakfast menu varied with the seasons, with heavier fare, such as pancakes fried in bacon fat, in the winter, and lighter meals, like cornflakes with fresh strawberries, in summer. My parents drank black coffee with breakfast, as they did with every meal, but we kids weren't allowed to have it until we were twelve or so.

MENU

FALL AND WINTER BREAKFAST

Cooked oatmeal topped with brown sugar and fresh milk

Toasted homemade bread, with butter and homemade strawberry jam

Thick bacon fried in the cast-iron skillet

Potatoes fried in bacon grease or lard

Eggs fried in bacon grease

Coffee

Milk for my brothers and me, especially in winter when the milk was cold

Spring and Summer Breakfast

Cornflakes and milk topped with strawberries, blueberries, or raspberries in season	*Thick slices of homemade bread covered with honey or homemade preserves*
Homemade sweet rolls (on weekends)	*Coffee*

Ma toasted slices of homemade bread on a toaster that required no electricity and stood directly on the warmest part of the cookstove. Sometimes, if the fire was down a bit and only coals remained, she removed a stove lid and replaced it with the toaster, which speeded up the toasting process considerably. The toaster, constructed of metal, was shaped like a pyramid, and would toast four slices of bread at a time. The slices had to be turned when the side facing the toaster was properly browned.

Toast made over the open coals had a very special taste, as the flavors of the homemade bread merged with those of the oak smoke. When the toasted bread was ready, we smeared it thick with butter and homemade jam—especially strawberry jam for me.

We usually had as many as a hundred chickens, and that meant we always had plenty of eggs. They were one of Ma's regular sources of income, which she spent on groceries, Christmas presents, and clothes for my brothers and me. But of course we also ate plenty of them. We all liked eggs—fried, sometimes poached, and occasionally hard-cooked. Fried eggs were a staple along with fried potatoes for breakfast. Seldom did Pa miss a day when he ate at least two of them. He always buried his fried eggs in a coat of black pepper. Pa liked pepper. When we helped Ma set the table for a meal, we made sure that the pepper shaker was in front of his place. There was a salt shaker, too, but as I recall we rarely used it, as Ma had already salted the food that required it before putting it on the table. Besides, many of the foods we ate used goodly amounts of salt in their preparation: sauerkraut, dill pickles, and smoked meats.

On winter weekends we had a little more time in the mornings, and when it was ten below zero and the snow was waist deep, Ma usually made a special breakfast. Of course, on most winter weekends, on top of the barn

Herman Apps and neighbor Louis Miller shoveling after a big snowfall

chores, we shoveled snow and cut or split wood for our ever-hungry wood-stoves. During heavy snowfalls the shoveling never seemed to stop, as we had to make sure paths were cleared from the house to the barn, from the barn to the pump house, from the pump house to the house, from the house to the chicken house, from the chicken house to the barn, from the granary to the barn and the chicken house, and from the house to the outhouse.

MENU

WEEKEND FALL AND WINTER BREAKFAST

Pancakes slathered with butter and drowned in syrup or sprinkled with brown sugar

Homemade strawberry, pineapple, or blueberry sweet rolls (with fruit preserves baked in)

Hot chocolate (on occasion)

Coffee

Milk

Buttermilk Pancakes

2 eggs
2 cups buttermilk
2 tablespoons butter, melted
2 cups flour
2 tablespoons sugar
2 tablespoons baking powder
1 teaspoon salt
1 teaspoon baking soda
Dash of nutmeg or cinnamon

In a large bowl, beat eggs. Add buttermilk and then melted butter. In a different bowl, sift together the flour, sugar, baking powder, salt, baking soda, and nutmeg or cinnamon. Add dry ingredients to the milk mixture and stir until just moistened. The batter will have lumps.

Lightly grease a griddle or skillet with butter or bacon fat and heat over medium heat. To test the griddle, sprinkle with a few drops of water. If the water drops sizzle around, the griddle is hot. Pour batter onto the griddle. Cook pancakes until they form bubbles and puff up. Turn and cook other side until golden brown.

Fried Potato Slices

    6 medium white or red potatoes
    2 tablespoons shortening or vegetable oil
    1 large onion, sliced (optional)
    Salt and pepper to taste
    2 tablespoons butter

Wash potatoes. Leave skins on and remove any eyes with a potato peeler. Cut into slices. Heat shortening or oil in a skillet until melted. Layer potato slices and onions, if using, in bottom of skillet. Sprinkle with salt and pepper. Continue layering potatoes. Dot butter on the top. Carefully turn potatoes while cooking so all sides brown.

Fried Eggs

Heat butter or bacon drippings in heavy skillet until hot enough to sizzle a drop of water. Break egg and slip carefully into the skillet to avoid breaking the yolk. While cooking, spoon butter over the egg until it sets for a "sunny-side-up" egg. Or, turn the egg over gently when whites are set for an "over-easy" egg.

CHAPTER 5

THE NOON MEAL

Dinner—as we called the meal served at noon—was the biggest meal of the day. Just like breakfast, it changed with the seasons, and of course dinner was considerably different during the school year when my brothers and I were at school and Ma and Pa ate on their own. Much of our summer dinner menu (and our suppers as well) came from the vegetable garden.

Herman, sons Donald and Darrel, and the farm dog, Fanny, outside the pump house, 1954

38

The garden season began with rhubarb and asparagus, and later included leaf lettuce, radishes, peas, strawberries, new potatoes, tomatoes, cucumbers, carrots, sweet corn, wild berries, early cabbage, late potatoes, pumpkin, and squash.

In fall our weekend tasks including helping with the corn harvest, making wood, and an assortment of other tasks as we made ready for winter on the farm—all of which left us very hungry for Ma's weekend dinners.

MENU

SUMMER DINNER

Freshly picked peas or beans, cooked until just tender

Freshly cut leaf lettuce drizzled with creamy dressing

New red potatoes boiled until fork-tender

Canned pork, chicken, or beef from the cellar

Homemade bread

Strawberry shortcake

MENU

FALL AND WINTER DINNER 1

Baked pork chops with sauerkraut

Home-canned peas or corn

Dill pickles

Homemade bread with butter

Apple pie made from fresh-picked apples

Milk and cheese

Coffee

MENU

FALL AND WINTER DINNER 2

Smoked ham cooked in milk sauce

Mashed potatoes with butter

Sweet-and-sour pickles

Cooked rutabagas

Homemade bread with butter and jam

Home-canned peaches

Milk and cheese

Coffee

Baked Pork Chops with Sauerkraut

8 pork chops
2 pounds sauerkraut, drained
1 large red apple, diced
1 onion, chopped
1 cup brown sugar

Preheat oven to 350 degrees. Heat a large skillet and brown the pork chops on both sides. Place the chops in a baking dish.

Mix the sauerkraut, apple, onion, and brown sugar in a bowl. Spread the sauerkraut mixture over the pork chops. Cover with foil. Bake until the pork is no longer pink inside, about 45 minutes.

Milk Sauce for Ham

⅓ cup vinegar
⅓ cup sugar
4 teaspoons dry mustard
3 egg yolks, beaten
1 pint cream or milk
Salt
Paprika

Heat vinegar in the top of a double boiler or in a metal mixing bowl set over a saucepan of simmering water. Stir in the sugar and dry mustard. Add beaten egg yolks. Add cream or milk. Cook slowly, stirring constantly, until mixture thickens, about 2 minutes. Salt to taste. Pour over baked ham. Sprinkle paprika on top.

Mashed Potatoes

4 pounds white potatoes
1 cup milk
¼ cup butter
1½ teaspoons salt
½ cup shredded cheddar cheese or ¼ cup sour cream (optional)

Peel the potatoes. Boil until soft and drain. Press the potatoes through a ricer or mash with a potato masher.

Heat the milk, butter, and salt together. Gradually whip the milk mixture into the potatoes until smooth and fluffy. The amount of milk will depend on the moisture in the potatoes, so add or use less accordingly. Stir in cheese or sour cream, if desired.

Note: If you are making gravy at the same time you are making mashed potatoes, save some of the potato water from boiling the potatoes to use in the gravy.

SCHOOL LUNCHES

Our school offered no hot lunch program, so we carried our lunches to school in empty Karo syrup pails or lard pails. (A few kids had fancy lunch pails.) Ma made our lunches before we left each morning. They usually consisted of a couple of jelly or peanut butter sandwiches, an apple, and a cookie or two or maybe a piece of chocolate cake. In winter, many of us brought along a jar of homemade soup, chili, or even some casserole left over from supper the night before. A pan of water sat on top of the schoolroom woodstove, both to provide humidity and to warm up those jars of food. Our teacher always reminded us to loosen the covers on the jars so they wouldn't explode and make a mess. I often thought it would be interesting to experience an exploding jar of chili, but it never happened.

I sometimes brought along a jar of chocolate milk—prepared before leaving home by mixing Hershey chocolate syrup with milk. Before going out for recess I would put my jar of soup in the pan on the stove, and then I would push my jar of chocolate milk into a snow bank near the school door. At lunchtime I had warm soup and cold milk. What more could one want?

Some of the poorer kids had little in their lunch pails, perhaps a slice of bread or two smeared with lard. We all ate our lunches together, outside on warm days and in the schoolroom during winter, and we often traded food items—a piece of cake for an apple; a jelly sandwich for a sugar cookie. And we shared some of our lunch with those kids who had next to nothing in their lunch pails.

OATMEAL COOKIES

2½ cups flour
2 teaspoons baking soda
1 teaspoon salt
2 cups butter, at room temperature
1½ cups white sugar
1½ cups brown sugar
4 eggs
2 teaspoons vanilla

6 cups old-fashioned oats
2 cups chocolate chips or raisins (optional)

Preheat oven to 375 degrees. In small bowl, combine flour, baking soda, and salt.

In a large bowl, beat the butter with the white sugar, then beat in the brown sugar, eggs, and vanilla until creamy. Gradually stir in the flour mixture. Stir in oats. Stir in chocolate chips or raisins, if desired. Drop by tablespoonsful onto ungreased cookie sheets. Bake until golden brown, 8 to 10 minutes.

CHAPTER 6

SUPPERTIME

In our home, it was unheard of for one of us to be absent from a meal—it occurred only when we were sick and in bed. It was in the evening, around the kitchen table, that we shared what was going on in school, with questions coming mostly from Ma as to whether we were keeping up with our homework, whether we were listening to and obeying the teacher, and how we were getting along with our schoolmates. Pa talked about farm work to be done. If it was autumn and we were in school, he talked about what had to

Herman holding baby Jerry

be done the coming weekend. In summer, he outlined what he had planned for the next day—making hay, hoeing potatoes, shocking grain, or whatever was happening on the farm at that time of the year.

We boys had our assigned chores, starting at a very young age. They included everything from carrying in water from the pump house to feeding the chickens and gathering eggs, carrying in wood, and taking out the ashes from our wood-burning stoves. When we were old enough to do barn chores, around six or seven, we helped with feeding calves, carrying in straw from the straw stack, throwing down hay from the haymow, and milking. If one of us had been shirking our everyday chores, Pa usually mentioned this privately rather than at the table, with a stern warning to do better.

Like our other daily meals, suppers varied considerably with the seasons. They were simple and largely centered on food fresh from the garden or, during the cold months, on food that Ma had canned and preserved during the summer and fall. We always had a bin of potatoes and another of rutabagas on the dirt floor under the house, plus many heads of cabbage, onions, and carrots, all of which appeared often on our table. The big crock of sauerkraut that sat in the pantry from fall until spring also figured into many meals. We butchered our own pork, so we had a ready supply of chops, bacon, and ham. During the fall hunting season, many of our meals featured squirrel and rabbit, and sometimes venison, if the deer hunt had been successful. On winter's most challenging days, we knew after trudging home from school in waist-deep snow that Ma would have something special waiting for us for supper, usually homemade vegetable soup with thick slices of freshly baked bread and her homemade jam.

MENU

Late Summer Supper

Boiled new potatoes

Sweet corn from the garden, boiled, with butter

Canned chicken baked in cream sauce

Homemade bread with butter

Wild berries

Coffee

RING BOLOGNA

We ate a lot of ring bologna when I was a kid, and every butcher shop we knew sold it. Ring bologna is made from a finely ground mixture of pork and beef, with a few spices added. The meat is stuffed into a casing about an inch and a half in diameter and is formed into a circle or ring. The ring resembles a horseshoe with heavy white twine tying the two ends together. The sausage is smoked and ready to eat without any further preparation, but the flavor is enhanced by frying or boiling. We ate it both ways, cooked and fried or simply sliced onto crackers or a piece of bread. When we traveled someplace and needed to pack a lunch, slices of ring bologna on saltine crackers was Pa's favorite.

RING BOLOGNA AND NAVY BEANS

2 cups dried navy beans
¼ cup brown sugar
3 tablespoons dark molasses
¼ cup ketchup
⅓ cup chopped onions
1 teaspoon salt
1 teaspoon prepared mustard
⅓ to ½ pound bacon, cooked and diced (optional)
1 ring bologna, sliced

Wash beans and removed any damaged ones. Place beans in a large bowl, cover with 4–6 cups of water, and soak overnight at room temperature.

Rinse and drain beans. Put them in a large pan and add enough water to cover. Bring to a boil, reduce heat, and cook for 20 to 25 minutes.

Preheat oven to 300 degrees. Put beans and liquid in a 2-quart casserole. Add remaining ingredients, except the ring bologna, and combine well. Cover and bake until beans are tender and flavors are blended, about 6 hours. In the last hour of cooking, add the bologna slices to the beans. Remove the cover for the last 30 minutes.

MENU

FALL AND WINTER SUPPER 1

Baked noodles with meat

Pickled beets

Boiled sauerkraut

Sliced cheese

Canned cherries

Coffee

Milk

MENU

FALL AND WINTER SUPPER 2

Fried ring bologna

Scalloped potatoes

Dill pickles

Cooked rutabagas

Homemade bread with butter and jam

Homemade canned applesauce

Coffee

Milk

Baked Noodles with Meat

1 package (12 ounces) egg noodles
1 onion
1 green pepper, cut fine
1 tablespoon fat
1 pound ground beef
2 cups vegetable soup (canned or homemade)
Salt and pepper to taste

Preheat oven to 375 degrees. Using package directions as your guide, boil the noodles in salted water until half done; drain and set aside. Fry the onion and pepper in the fat in a large skillet. Add the ground beef and cook until it loses its red color. Add soup and cooked noodles. Season to taste with salt and pepper. Put in a 1½-quart casserole dish and bake for 1 hour.

Note: Leftover meats can be ground and used in place of the ground beef.

Macaroni with Ham Hotdish

2 cups cooked elbow noodles
2 cups minced ham
2 cups creamed corn
1 cup bread crumbs
Butter
Salt and pepper to taste

Preheat oven to 400 degrees. Grease a baking dish with butter. Arrange cooked noodles, ham, and corn in alternating layers in the baking dish. Cover with bread crumbs and dot with butter. Add salt and pepper to taste. Bake until crumbs are brown, 20 to 30 minutes.

Scalloped Potatoes

6–7 medium potatoes
4 tablespoons butter, divided
3 tablespoons flour
Salt and pepper to taste
2–4 cups milk
1 onion, chopped

Preheat oven to 350 degrees. Wash, pare, and cut potatoes in ¼-inch slices. Heat 3 tablespoons butter in skillet until melted. Mix in flour, salt, and pepper. Stir constantly over low heat until mixture is smooth. Remove from heat and add enough milk to make a creamy white sauce. Return to the heat and stir constantly until boiling; boil for 1 minute.

Put a layer of potatoes in buttered baking dish or shallow pan. Add a layer of white sauce and some of the onion. Repeat with another layer of potatoes, white sauce, and onion. Repeat layering. Sprinkle with salt and pepper. Dot with remaining 1 tablespoon butter. Cover and bake for 25 minutes. Uncover and bake until potatoes are soft and golden brown, about 1 hour.

Bean Salad

1 can (16 ounces) green beans, drained
1 can (16 ounces) yellow beans, drained
1 can (16 ounces) kidney beans, drained and rinsed
1 can (16 ounces) garbanzo beans, drained and rinsed
1 medium onion, chopped
1 medium green pepper, chopped
¾ cup sugar
⅔ cup white vinegar
⅓ cup oil
1 teaspoon salt
½ teaspoon pepper

Mix all the beans with onion and green pepper in a large bowl. In another bowl, whisk sugar, vinegar, oil, salt, and pepper. Pour over the bean mixture. Lightly stir all ingredients together. Refrigerate. Tastes even better the next day.

Rutabaga and Potato Casserole

2 medium potatoes
2 medium rutabagas
½ cup flour
1 teaspoon baking powder
1 teaspoon salt
⅛ teaspoon pepper
4 eggs, beaten
¼ cup milk
¼ cup butter, melted, or drippings

Preheat oven to 325 degrees. Peel potatoes and rutabagas. Grate them and let sit in a bit of water.

Stir together the flour, baking powder, salt, and pepper in a large bowl. Take out half of the flour mixture and set aside. Blend the beaten eggs into the flour mixture remaining in the bowl. Add the milk and butter and stir.

Drain the potatoes and rutabagas. Add the other half of the dry flour mixture to the potatoes and rutabagas and stir. Add the floured vegetables to the egg and milk mixture. Place in a greased 1-quart casserole. Bake for 1 hour.

Beef Vegetable Soup

3 pounds meaty beef chuck bones
4 onions, chopped
1 small head of cabbage, cut up
3 ribs of celery, chopped
1 can (16 ounces) tomatoes (Eleanor would have used her own
    canned tomatoes.)
1 can (10 ounces) tomato soup
1 bay leaf
1 tablespoon sugar
4 medium potatoes, cut up
1 cup canned peas
Salt and pepper to taste

Place meat bones and onions in a large pot or soup kettle. Add enough cold water to cover. Cover and bring to a boil, then reduce the heat to simmer. Cook slowly for 2 hours.

Remove the meat from the bones and skim off the fat. Set meat aside. Add cabbage, celery, tomatoes, soup, bay leaf, and sugar to the pot. Cover and simmer for 1 hour.

Return the meat to the pot along with the potatoes and cook for 15 minutes. Add the peas and simmer another 10 minutes. Season to taste with salt and pepper.

CHAPTER 7

MAKING DO

I was born in July of 1934, and thus my childhood straddled the Great Depression (1929–1941) and the World War II years (1941–1945). The Great Depression caused untold misery for city and country folks alike. When the banks closed, my parents lost the money they had been saving to make a down payment on the home farm, which they were renting. Their income from the sale of milk, hogs, and potatoes plummeted. But unlike many urban people who lost their jobs and were often hungry, farmers almost always had something to eat, because we grew most of our own food. Ma also somehow managed to obtain such staples as coffee and sugar, either purchasing them or trading for them with eggs and other farm produce.

The 1930s also brought severe drought to the West and Midwest, and just as the western and southwestern states suffered through the Dust Bowl, so did Wisconsin. The crops grown on the sandy soils of our home farm were but a shadow of what we produced in years with adequate rain. The hay crop, essential for feeding the cattle through the long winter months, was slight, and the summer pastures that the cattle depended on dried up by August, forcing Pa to feed the cows some of the scarce hay crop. To make matters even worse, a dry wind blew from the southwest, day after agonizing day, filling the air with clouds of dirty, yellow dust and tearing up the soil on newly plowed fields.

I remember a day in the late 1930s when a man stopped by the farm and knocked on the door. He wore torn and dirty clothes and an old felt hat, and he walked kind of bent over. When Ma answered the door, the man said in a low, quiet voice that he was willing to work for something to eat. Ma invited him

Jerry and Buster

in, sat him down at the kitchen table, and made him a thick cheese sandwich, which he hurriedly ate.

I had not known about men like this, who had lost their jobs and were riding the freight trains from town to town, in search of work and something to eat. But Ma and Pa had. As Ma poured the man a glass of milk, she told him that he didn't need to do any work for us. She even made another sandwich and packed it with a couple of cookies to take with him. With tears in his eyes, the man thanked Ma for what she had done. I watched him trudge down the country road, no doubt hoping to find another kind person who would give him food or work.

I do not recall being hungry during the Depression, as we always had a huge garden that we depended on during good years and bad. We did have to make do with the clothes and shoes we had, as every spare nickel— the meager income from our small herd of cattle, the few dollars' worth of eggs my mother sold and traded for groceries at the Mercantile, and the money from our twenty-acre potato field—went to keep us on the farm, ever hopeful that better days would come.

Ma made do in many ways during those trying years, and no food went to waste. She was a master of preparing leftovers in a variety of ways, from using leftover meat and vegetables in soup to creating tasty hotdishes of

MA'S APRON

About the only time Ma didn't wear an apron was when she went to town for grocery shopping or to church on Sunday. Otherwise, every morning after putting on her dress, she pulled on her apron. It was a full-length affair, with a cloth strap that went over her head and strings that tied in the back, the front of it covering most of her dress. The apron had two pockets in front, large enough to hold a notepad and pencil, a handkerchief, safety pins, perhaps thread, and a needle stuck in a piece of fabric, all of which Ma called into use throughout her day.

Ma would never think of buying an apron; she always made her own, usually from feed sacks. During the Depression years, when money was scarce, homemakers turned these empty bags into practical items, not only aprons but dishcloths and even dresses. Savvy feed companies began printing feed sacks with bright colors, and some printed them with the fronts and backs of stuffed toys. (My first teddy bear was printed on a feed sack. Ma cut out the pieces, sewed them together, and stuffed the bear with quilt batting.)

Jerry with his feed sack bear

Ma had several aprons, some badly worn and thin after many years of use and some newer and more colorful that she wore only when company came. Her apron had multiple uses besides protecting a dress from spills and splashes. Ma gathered up the corners of her apron to tote vegetables gathered in the garden, carry eggs from the chicken house, haul kindling wood from the woodpile, and wipe a tear from one of my brother's eyes when he fell and skinned his knee. She used it to dry her hands when the Watkins man came knocking on the kitchen door or to dab at her sweating forehead as she worked over the hot stove. If she wanted to capture Pa's attention when he was working in a field some distance from the house, she'd stand in front of the house and swing her apron in a big circle.

many kinds. She used up end-of-season produce in her homemade chili sauce, which she used to add flavor to chili, meat loaf, and casseroles. With bread that was a few days old, she made bread pudding, not wasting a single slice. Likewise, she sewed patch upon patch on our worn overalls and shirts and darned the holes in our socks. Nothing was discarded in those days—no morsel of food or item of clothing wasted.

On December 7, 1941, the United States entered World War II, and farm prices that had been rock bottom during the Depression began to improve. But rationing presented a new set of challenges. The government issued ration books to every person, adults and children alike, limiting purchases of gasoline, tires, shoes, rubber footwear, and many food items, including meat, sugar, coffee, and canned goods.

We raised our own hogs and grew a huge garden, so those items were not problems for us. The biggest hardship my mother faced was sugar rationing. She was unable to purchase the amount of sugar she needed for baking, so she turned to an alternative source of sweetener: sorghum syrup.

We grew up to two acres of sweet sorghum during the war years. Harry Korleski, who owned and operated a water-powered sorghum mill nearby, made syrup by running the sorghum stalks through the mill to squeeze out the juice and then boiling down the juice. My mother canned it, stored it in the cellar, and used it in a variety of recipes.

When the war ended in 1945, great changes occurred on farms. That year Pa bought our first tractor. But he also kept our team of horses, as he never quite trusted a tractor to be as dependable as his faithful team. When sugar was again available for purchase, Ma bought two hundred pounds, storing a hundred pounds in our attic. "I don't want to run out of sugar ever again," she said. The summer of 1945 was the last that we grew sweet sorghum, even though Ma continued to buy some each year from neighbors who grew it. The family had developed a taste for sorghum cookies.

Chili Sauce

8 onions
8 green bell peppers
2 red bell peppers
24 tomatoes, cored and cut up
1½ cups sugar
2 tablespoons salt
1 tablespoon cloves
1 tablespoon cinnamon
1 tablespoon allspice
½ cup vinegar

Grind up the onions, green peppers, and red peppers. In a large pot, combine ground onions and peppers, tomatoes, sugar, salt, cloves, cinnamon, and allspice and simmer for 1½ hours. Add vinegar and simmer ½ hour longer. Store in the refrigerator in covered containers.

Leftover Chicken Hotdish

6 cups uncooked egg noodles
2 tablespoons butter
2 tablespoons flour
1 teaspoon salt
¼ teaspoon pepper
2 cups milk
Sour cream (optional)
3 cups diced leftover cooked chicken
1 cup diced celery (optional)
About 20 butter-flavored crackers, crushed

Preheat oven to 350 degrees. Cook noodles until tender and drain. Melt butter over low heat in a skillet and add flour, salt, and pepper. Stir well. Add milk slowly and stir until smooth. Stir in sour cream if you have some. In a baking dish, alternate noodles, white sauce, and chicken in layers. Add celery, if desired. Sprinkle crushed crackers on top. Bake for 30 minutes.

Creamed Peas and Potatoes

2 cups new peas
4 medium potatoes, peeled and cut into 1-inch pieces
2 cups cream
1 tablespoon cornstarch
1 tablespoon flour
1 tablespoon butter, melted
Parsley or paprika for garnish

Cook fresh-picked peas in a pan with a small amount of water until just tender. Cook the potatoes in a separate pan. Drain the vegetables and combine.

Bring the cream, cornstarch, flour, and melted butter to a boil in a pan, stirring constantly over low heat. Remove sauce from heat and add to the vegetables. Sprinkle the top with parsley or paprika for garnish.

Baking Powder Biscuits

2 cups flour
4 teaspoons baking powder
½ teaspoon salt
4 tablespoons butter or other shortening
¾–1 cup milk

Preheat oven to 400–425 degrees. Sift flour, baking powder, and salt into a mixing bowl. Add shortening and blend with a pastry blender or rub in with the tips of your fingers. Add milk gradually, cutting in with a knife, until mixture rounds up into a soft, smooth dough. Roll out the dough ½-inch thick on a lightly floured board (do not use too much flour). Cut out with a floured biscuit cutter. Bake on a greased baking sheet until browned, about 15 minutes. Best served hot from the oven.

Note: For pot pie crust, roll dough ½-inch thick, lay over casserole, and press edges to the dish. Make a slit in the top. For drop biscuits, add an additional 1 cup milk and form drop biscuits on baking sheet. Bake as for rolled biscuits.

Bread Pudding with Good Stuff

6 slices dry (day-old) bread
1 pint cream or milk
½ cup sugar
4 tablespoons butter, melted
4 eggs, beaten
¼ teaspoon cinnamon
½ teaspoon vanilla
¼ teaspoon salt
Raisins
"Good Stuff" for topping (recipe follows)

Preheat oven to 350 degrees. Soak bread in cream or milk about 20 minutes. Add sugar, butter, eggs, cinnamon, vanilla, and salt. Add raisins. Put in a buttered baking dish and set the dish in a pan of hot water. Bake until a knife inserted in the pudding comes out clean, 30 to 40 minutes. Serve with "Good Stuff" on top. (Good Stuff is what the Apps boys called it.)

Good Stuff

¾ cup sugar
2 tablespoons cornstarch
Pinch of salt
1 cup water
1 teaspoon lemon extract

Combine the sugar, cornstarch, and salt in a pan. Add water and lemon extract. Heat over medium heat until mixture comes to a boil. Reduce the heat and simmer, stirring constantly for 1 minute. Pour over bread pudding.

Sorghum Cookies

1 cup sugar, plus more for dipping dough before baking
¾ cup shortening, melted
⅓ cup sorghum syrup
1 egg
2 cups flour
2 teaspoons baking soda
1 teaspoon cinnamon
1 teaspoon cloves
½ teaspoon ginger

Combine sugar and melted shortening in a mixing bowl and beat until creamy. Let cool for 10 minutes. Add sorghum and egg to sugar mixture. In another bowl, combine flour, baking soda, cinnamon, cloves, and ginger. Stir into sugar and egg mixture. Cover the dough and refrigerate for 30 minutes.

Preheat oven to 350 degrees and grease a cookie sheet. Roll chilled dough into balls the size of walnuts, dip in sugar, and place on cookie sheet 2 inches apart. Bake until edges look brown, about 7 minutes. Let cool 1 minute on cookie sheet and then transfer to a wire cooling rack.

Sorghum Pumpkin Muffins

2 cups flour
2 teaspoons cinnamon
1 teaspoon baking soda
½ teaspoon nutmeg
¼ teaspoon ground cloves
¼ teaspoon salt
¼ cup brown sugar
½ cup oil
2 eggs
1 cup sorghum syrup
½ cup canned pumpkin or home-cooked pumpkin
½ teaspoon vanilla

TOPPING
½ cup flour
¼ cup butter, softened
¼ cup brown sugar
½ teaspoon cinnamon

Preheat oven to 350 degrees and grease a 12-cup muffin tin. In a medium bowl, stir together 2 cups flour, 2 teaspoons cinnamon, baking soda, nutmeg, cloves, and salt. Set aside. In a large bowl, combine ¼ cup brown sugar, oil, and eggs. Add sorghum, pumpkin, and vanilla and stir. Gradually stir in the flour mixture, about one-third at a time, until just combined. Do not overmix. Fill the 12 muffin cups to half full.

To make the topping, combine flour, brown sugar, butter, and cinnamon until ingredients are mixed. The mixture will be crumbly. Sprinkle topping over muffins and bake until a toothpick inserted in the center comes out clean, about 25 minutes.

Sorghum Cake

¾ cup sorghum syrup
¾ cup brown sugar
½ cup shortening
1 teaspoon vanilla
2 eggs, beaten
3 cups cake flour
1 tablespoon baking powder
½ teaspoon baking soda
½ teaspoon salt
½ cup milk
Eleanor's Icing (recipe follows)

Preheat oven to 350 degrees and grease two 9-inch round cake pans. Beat sorghum syrup, brown sugar, shortening, and vanilla in a large bowl until creamy. Add eggs and beat well. In another bowl, mix the flour, baking powder, baking soda, and salt. Add the flour mixture to the egg mixture alternately with the milk. Pour the cake batter into pans and bake for 45 minutes. Frost when cool.

Eleanor's Icing

1½ cups sugar
½ cup water
1 tablespoon light corn syrup
½ teaspoon salt
2 egg whites
1 teaspoon vanilla

Cook sugar, water, corn syrup, and salt in a saucepan over low heat, stirring constantly, until sugar is dissolved. Cover the pan and boil for 3 minutes. Then, to test for readiness, use a teaspoon to drop a small amount of the sugar liquid into a cup of cold water. When it is ready, it will form a small ball. Beat egg whites in a medium bowl until stiff. Remove syrup from heat and pour slowly over egg whites, beating constantly. Add vanilla. Continue beating until it is spreading consistency.

Sugarless Cake Frosting

1 square unsweetened chocolate
½ of a 14-ounce can of sweetened condensed milk
A few grains of salt
1 teaspoon vanilla
½ tablespoon hot water

Melt the chocolate in a double boiler or in a metal mixing bowl set over a saucepan of simmering water. Stir in half a can of sweetened condensed milk and salt. Stir and cook over boiling water until it is thick, about 5 minutes.

Remove from heat. Stir in vanilla. Then stir in the hot water. Add a few more drops of hot water if it is too thick.

Victory Spice Cake

2 cups cake flour
2 teaspoons baking powder
1½ teaspoons allspice
¾ teaspoon salt
½ cup shortening
1 teaspoon grated lemon rind
¾ cup honey
2 egg yolks
½ cup milk
⅔ cup chopped raisins
1 teaspoon vanilla
2 egg whites
⅓ cup chopped walnuts

Preheat the oven to 350 degrees and grease an 8-inch-square cake pan. In a large bowl, mix together the flour, baking powder, allspice, and salt. In another bowl, beat the shortening with the lemon rind until creamy. Add the honey to the shortening a little at a time and beat well after each addition. Gradually add one-quarter of the flour mixture to the honey mixture. Add egg yolks, one at a time, mixing well each time. Add the remaining flour mixture a bit at time, alternating with the milk, and mix well. Stir in the raisins and vanilla.

Beat the egg whites until stiff and stir thoroughly into the batter. Pour the batter into pan. Sprinkle the walnuts on top. Bake until a toothpick inserted in the center comes out clean, about 50 minutes.

VICTORY GARDENS

During World War II the US government encouraged citizens to grow "Victory Gardens" as a way of producing their own food. As many as twenty million citizens, urban and rural people alike, planted gardens in vacant lots and backyards. Gardens were not a new idea for farm people, of course, and my mother never referred to her large plot as a Victory Garden.

Magazines such as the *Saturday Evening Post* and *Life* ran stories about growing and preserving garden produce. Just as farm people had done for years, urban gardeners were encouraged to can their own produce so commercially canned fruits and vegetables would be available for the troops. According to the National WWII Museum, Victory Gardens produced more than a million tons of vegetables during the war.

PART TWO

EVERYDAY FOODS

CHAPTER 8

THE CHICKEN AND THE EGG

The cycle began with a call from the depot agent in Wild Rose in early April informing Ma that our chicks had arrived on the morning train and that we should stop by as soon as possible to pick them up. Ma had ordered them from a chicken hatchery in the southern part of the state: one hundred layers (egg-producing chickens) of the White Leghorn variety and fifty White Plymouth Rock broilers (chickens raised for meat).

Pa brought the little chicks home in large cardboard boxes divided into sections, with a dozen or so chicks in each section. He carried the boxes into the kitchen and placed them by the kitchen stove, one of the few warm places on the farm. Meanwhile, after the brooder house had been scrubbed and swept, Pa started the brooder stove, a wood- and coal-burning stove with a large tin canopy under which the little chicks could gather to keep warm. He filled the metal feeding troughs with chick feed and filled the glass water jars, which were specially designed so the chicks could easily drink. With the brooder house ready, he carried the chicks from the kitchen to their new home.

The chicks grew rapidly, and when they were about four weeks old, if the weather was mild, they were allowed outside in a small fenced-in grassy area adjacent to the brooder house. When the layers were about five months old, they would find a home in the chicken house, a low, one-story building with tall windows facing south and located just west of the farmhouse. The broilers were of both sexes, but the layers had been sexed, meaning there were supposed to be no roosters. But sexing baby chicks was as much an art as it was a science, and a few little roosters always made their way into

CHICKEN VARIETIES

We raised three varieties of chickens: one for eggs, one for meat, and one just to look at and listen to. Laying hens were smaller than those raised for meat. Popular egg-producing breeds when I was growing up were White Leghorns, which laid white eggs, and Rhode Island Reds, which laid brown eggs. In those years the market was stronger for white eggs, so Ma raised only White Leghorns. Leghorn layers could also be expected to lay from 280 to 300 eggs per year, on average.

The broiler breed that Ma preferred was White Plymouth Rock. They did well on our farm, and they grew fast, usually ready for market about two months from the time they were little chicks falling over each other in the brooder house.

Pa enjoyed having a few bantam roosters around. They were colorful, in several shades of brown, bronze, and orange, and each had his own personality. Although they were usually only half the size of White Leghorn roosters, they did not let their size get in the way of their prowess. They strutted around the chicken yard liked they owned the place; the layers mostly ignored them. Occasionally a Leghorn rooster would stand up to a cocky little bantam rooster. The results were usually a draw. Confidence goes a long way in a rooster fight, and the little bantams had an over-abundance of confidence.

the chicken flock. The broilers remained in the brooder house until they were large enough for butchering.

The chickens were Ma's project. She supervised the cleaning and disinfecting of the brooder house and enlisted Pa to buy the chick feed and, later, a special layer mash for the hens that encouraged egg production. She kept records of the kinds of feed purchased, the cost, and the income from the sale of eggs and broilers.

We all helped Ma with the chickens. My brothers and I gathered eggs each day. One of us fed and watered the growing chicks in the brooder house, and one of us was assigned to feed and haul water for the laying hens each afternoon. We laid cobs of corn on a large block of stovewood, chopped them into little pieces with a hatchet, and then fed the chopped cob corn to the layers, along with oats and layer mash.

The broilers would be butchered when they reached seven to nine weeks of age. Ma traded the dressed broilers for groceries at the Wild Rose Mercantile, but she always kept a few live ones for our own use and for relatives who came to visit. When we were expecting visitors on a Sunday, we butchered a broiler or two on Saturday afternoon. Ma believed that the flavor of fresh-butchered meat far exceeded that of anything purchased in a butcher shop or grocery store.

A laying hen, properly fed and cared for, could be expected to produce eggs for three to four years. Ma knew the age of the chickens in her flock because she placed a ring on each one's leg when she moved them from the brooder house to the chicken house. Each year the ring was a different color—red, blue, green, yellow. By looking at the rings she knew how old the chicken was and whether its egg-producing years were waning.

Each fall, usually on a Saturday, we had a chicken butchering day at the farm. The previous evening, when the chickens were all on their roosts in the chicken house, Ma and Pa would enter with a chicken hook—a wooden pole about five feet long with a stiff wire hook on the end. When Ma pointed to a chicken, Pa slipped the hook over the chicken's leg and captured it. Its egg-laying days were over. Pa put the captured chickens into a wire crate, one after the other, as Ma pointed out the ones that she deemed destined for the cook pot. On a particular night, as many as twenty-five or more old layers might be selected.

The following day, when the morning barn chores were finished, we began butchering the old layers. We all had a job to do. One of us cut the heads off the chickens, using the same hatchet and chopping block that we'd used to prepare their corn. Another was in charge of digging into the crate for the next chicken. Meanwhile, the headless chickens, much to the surprise and horror of any city cousin who might be visiting, ran in circles before falling dead. One of my brothers gathered up the dead chickens and carried them to where Pa had a pail filled with boiling water, the feather-plucking station. He immersed the carcass in the boiling water, pulled it out, and plucked off wet feathers that accumulated at his feet. When the chickens were free of feathers, Pa put them in a big wash pan and carried them into the house, where Ma was waiting at the kitchen table to remove the entrails, saving the livers and hearts in the process.

When all of the chickens were butchered, Pa and Ma cut the meat into chunks that would fit into canning jars. For the next couple of days, the kitchen

CHICKEN TERMS

- **Broilers and fryers:** Hens and roosters seven to nine weeks old and weighing about three pounds
- **Roasters:** Hens and roosters up to eight months old and weighing up to five pounds
- **Stewing chickens:** Hens no longer laying eggs and usually more than a year old. May weigh up to six or seven pounds. Meat is tougher than that of younger chickens.
- **Capons:** Castrated roosters. Tender and flavorful meat. Best when roasted.

was filled with the smell of chicken. Ma spent up to eight hours canning the chicken, laboring over the steaming kettle and lifting the jars to cool on the kitchen table before storing them on shelves in the cellar. All winter we feasted on chicken soup, fried chicken, and the occasional chicken casserole. The next April we would once more hear the peeping of little chicks, and the cycle would begin again.

Eggs were also an important part of our diet on the farm, a staple in our breakfasts and important for Ma's baking. They were a dependable source of income as well, supplementing what we earned from the milk we sold, the crops we peddled, and the cash crops, such as potatoes and cucumbers. Ma traded eggs for groceries at the Mercantile in Wild Rose on Saturday night when we went to town. And she sold the excess eggs (at about thirty cents a dozen) to the egg man who made the rounds of the neighborhood with his truck once a week or so. The egg man paid cash on the spot. Ma used her "egg money" to buy Christmas and birthday presents and occasionally new clothes and shoes.

George and Mable Renkert, longtime friends of my mother who lived in Chicago, provided another market for Ma's extra eggs. Every few weeks, she shipped them six dozen eggs in a wooden crate. My brothers and I looked forward to the return of the empty egg crate, which the Renkerts filled with comics from the *Chicago Tribune*. When the egg crate arrived, we hurried through our chores and then settled into reading the exploits of Dick Tracy, Flash Gordon, Joe Palooka, Jungle Jim, and the Phantom.

Roast Chicken

Preheat oven to 400 degrees. Rinse the chicken with cool water. Dry with cloth or paper towels. Loosen the skin and rub the cavity of the chicken with salt if desired. (Use ½ teaspoon salt for each pound of chicken; do not salt the inside if you are using stuffing.) Rub the salt all over the outside of the chicken, including under the skin.

The rule of thumb is to allow 1 cup of stuffing to every pound of bird. (You can also bake the stuffing in a casserole separate from the bird. If it dries out, moisten it with chicken broth.) Stuff the chicken just before roasting, not ahead of time. Fill wishbone area of chicken with stuffing first. Close the cavity with a skewer. Fold the neck skin over back. Fasten with a skewer if necessary. Fold the wings back with tips touching and tie together with kitchen string. Tie the drumsticks to the tail.

Place the chicken breast side up on a rack in a shallow roasting pan. Brush the entire chicken with melted butter. No need to cover. Pour some chicken broth in the bottom of the pan.

Roast the chicken in the oven until brown, 1¾ to 2½ hours depending on the size. Spoon some of the pan juices over the chicken while roasting.

When chicken is two-thirds done, cut the string between the drumsticks to test for doneness. Chicken is done when the drumstick meat is soft and you can pull the drumstick up and down easily. (Use something to protect your fingers from the heat.) After taking the chicken out of the oven, let it rest for at least 10 minutes before carving.

Stuffing

Cook 3 tablespoons chopped onion in 2–3 tablespoons butter over low heat until it softens.

Combine onion and butter with 4 cups dry bread cubes, 1 teaspoon salt, ¼ teaspoon pepper, ¼ teaspoon poultry seasoning, and sage to taste. Add enough chicken broth to moisten. Toss to mix. This recipe makes enough for a 4-pound bird.

Giblets

Combine giblets from 1 chicken with a small onion, a celery rib, and some salt and pepper. Cover with water and cook until tender. Add other seasonings to taste. Cooking time varies depending on the age of the bird and the size. Remove the liver after cooking 20 minutes. Add the strained broth to your gravy. Use a food chopper to chop the cooked giblets and add them to the gravy.

Canned Chicken

Have all jars, lids, rings, and canning equipment thoroughly clean and in good condition.

Steam or boil a whole chicken until about two-thirds done. Remove all of the skin and bones. Pack the meat into hot, sterile jars, leaving 1-inch headspace. Add ½ teaspoon salt per pint jar or 1 teaspoon salt per quart jar.

Skim fat from broth. Bring the broth to a boil. Pour boiling broth over the chicken, leaving 1-inch headspace. Remove air bubbles by slipping a knife into the sides of the jars. Wipe the top of the jar before covering with the seal and lid. Process the pint jars for 1 hour and 15 minutes. Process quart jars for 1 hour and 30 minutes.

Carefully follow all safety and nutrition directions included with your jars and consult other canning resources if necessary. When using a pressure canner, follow all directions given by the manufacturer. Food products must be held at high temperature, 10 pounds pressure, to kill bacteria and prevent spoilage. For good basic instructions on canning and preserving, see *Ball Complete Book of Home Preserving*, edited by Judi Kingry and Lauren Devine (Toronto: Robert Rose, 2006).

Chicken Stock

4- or 5-pound chicken
1 peeled carrot
1 rib celery
1 medium onion
1 bay leaf
1 teaspoon salt
⅛ teaspoon pepper
2 sprigs of parsley
Celery salt or onion seasoning to taste

Clean chicken and remove skin and fat. Place chicken in a kettle with all vegetables, seasonings, and herbs. Add enough water to cover the chicken completely. Bring water to a boil. Reduce heat, cover, and simmer until the chicken is tender, up to 2 hours.

Remove chicken from the kettle; remove meat from the bones and refrigerate for other use. Return bones to the broth and simmer for another 45 minutes. Strain the broth with clean cheesecloth. To remove the fat from broth, skim it off with a spoon, or lay a paper towel on the surface of the top to soak off the fat, repeating with more paper towels until fat is removed. If possible, put the kettle in a cool place or refrigerate overnight. In the morning you can lift off the fat with a spoon.

Chicken stock should be cooled before storing in the refrigerator or freezer. Pour the stock into containers and let sit for 30 minutes, then refrigerate. If freezing, leave at least 1-inch headspace to allow for expansion.

Chicken Soup

1 fresh chicken, cleaned, skin removed, and cut into pieces
1 teaspoon salt
½ cup chopped celery
½ cup chopped carrots
6 medium potatoes, cubed (can substitute chopped rutabagas
    or turnips)
1 medium onion, chopped
Salt and pepper
Cooked noodles (optional)

Place cut-up chicken in a large pot of water, enough to almost cover it. Add the salt. Bring to a boil and then simmer until chicken is tender, about 1 hour. If needed, skim fat off the top. Remove the chicken from the broth. Take the meat off the bones. Cut some into 1-inch pieces for the soup. Refrigerate some for another recipe.

If liquid seems too thick, add water to the broth. Add the celery, carrots, potatoes, and onion. Season with salt and pepper to taste. Bring to a boil again. Lower the heat and simmer until the vegetables are soft. Then add as much cooked chicken as you like. Add cooked noodles to the soup, if desired.

Deviled Eggs

6 hard-cooked eggs, peeled and rinsed
3 tablespoons mayonnaise
½ teaspoon white vinegar
½ teaspoon dry mustard
¼ teaspoon salt
¼ teaspoon pepper
Lettuce leaves and paprika, for serving

Carefully cut hard-cooked eggs in half lengthwise. Use a spoon to slip out the yellow yolks. Mash the yolks with a fork in a bowl. Mix in mayonnaise, vinegar, mustard, salt, and pepper. Fill each egg half with the yolk mixture. Arrange lettuce on a platter. Put eggs on top of lettuce. Sprinkle with paprika.

Egg Salad Sandwich

4 hard-cooked eggs, peeled and rinsed
Salt and pepper to taste
1 tablespoon mayonnaise
Pickle relish to taste
Buttered bread slices and lettuce leaves, for serving

Slice the eggs in half; remove yolks and set aside. Chop the whites. Force the yolks through a potato ricer. Gently mix yolks and whites and season with salt and pepper. Moisten the egg mixture with mayonnaise and a bit of pickle relish. Spread mixture on buttered bread and top with lettuce.

CHAPTER 9

MILK, BUTTER, AND CHEESE

With our small herd of dairy cows producing about forty gallons of milk a day, we had all the milk we wanted to drink. The milkman picked up nearly all of it, except for the few quarts that my mother saved for our family. Unfortunately, in summer the icebox did not chill milk enough to make it taste the best, so we drank milk mainly in winter. Ma used lots of milk in her cooking and baking throughout the year.

Every day, the milkman came to pick up our milk and transport it to the cheese factory. Nearly all of the milk that we shipped to the factory was made into cheddar cheese, with a little of the cream churned into butter. When the milkman came to collect our milk, he delivered our order of cheese and butter from the factory, and the cost of those items was subtracted from the milk checks we received every two weeks from the cheese factory. I don't recall my mother ever buying butter or cheese from the grocery store. And I don't recall that we ate any cheese other than the cheddar made at the cheese factory where we shipped our milk.

Each evening, after the cows were milked and the two or three ten-gallon cans of fresh milk toted to the pump house for cooling, we'd carry in a small pail of milk for drinking and for Ma's use in cooking. We put the milk in the icebox to cool during the summer and to keep from freezing in the winter (in winter, by morning the temperature in the house often dipped well below freezing). Ma also liked to skim some cream from the top of the milk in the milk cans to use for whipped cream and other recipes that called for cream. Pa frowned on this cream skimming because the cheese factory paid for milk based on its butterfat content—the amount of cream in the milk.

81

Herman at milking time

He tried to keep the butterfat in the milk at about 3.5 percent, a good average butterfat level for milk from Holstein cows. Guernsey and Jersey cows give less milk than Holsteins, but the butterfat content is higher, sometimes as high as 5.5 percent for Jerseys.

During ordinary weather, the milkman came every day and picked up four ten-gallon cans of milk (less in the cold months), the result of our evening and morning milkings. But when a blizzard blocked the roads and the milkman couldn't reach our farm, we poured the milk into our four spare cans—and eventually into pots, pans, the copper boiler, and any other vessel that could hold the milk until the snowplow cleared the way so the milk-man's truck could get through.

HOW TO MAKE BUTTER

1. Start with a clean, clear canning jar with a sturdy lid.
2. Fill the jar about one-third full of cream.
3. Shake the jar vigorously until butter forms—may take ten to fifteen minutes.
4. Separate the butter from the buttermilk by straining it through a colander or a piece of cheesecloth.
5. Wash the butter with cold water, gently turning the butter with a spoon until the water runs clear.
6. Mix in a little salt, to taste. Or leave unsalted.
7. Put butter in a cool place for an hour or two and it's ready to eat.
8. What's left behind is buttermilk. It is a nutritious drink, though perhaps an acquired taste. It can also be used in cooking.

Buttermilk Biscuits

2 cups flour
3 teaspoons baking powder
¼ teaspoon baking soda
½ teaspoon salt
5 tablespoons shortening
1 cup buttermilk

Preheat oven to 450 degrees and flour a flat surface. Mix the flour, baking powder, baking soda, and salt in a large bowl. Cut in the shortening with a fork until the mixture is crumbly. Gradually add the buttermilk and stir until the dough thickens.

Put the dough on the floured surface and knead for 30 seconds. Roll out the dough until it is ½-inch thick. Cut into biscuits. Bake on an ungreased cookie sheet until golden brown, 12 to 15 minutes.

Fresh Peas in Milk Sauce

4 cups fresh shelled peas
2 teaspoons sugar
1 teaspoon salt
1 small green onion, chopped
2 tablespoons butter
1 cup cream or milk
⅛ teaspoon pepper

Put peas in a pot. Add sugar, salt, onion, and enough water to cover the peas. Cook over medium heat until peas are tender, 5 minutes. Drain the water. Add the butter and turn the heat to very low so the butter melts. Add cream or milk and pepper. Heat through on very low heat, just to warm the milk but not so that it cooks.

Homemade Cottage Cheese

2 quarts skim milk
¼ cup plus 2 tablespoons white vinegar
¼ teaspoon salt
¼ cup whole milk

Pour the skim milk in a saucepan and heat it until it reads 120 degrees on a candy thermometer. Remove from the heat. Add the vinegar and mix slowly for 2 minutes. Cover the pan with a cloth and let rest for a half hour.

By now cottage cheese curds will have formed. Pour the mixture of curds and whey into a colander lined with a thin cheesecloth and let drain for 3 minutes. Lift the curds from the colander with the cheesecloth and run cold water over the curds, squeezing the curds in the cloth until they are cool. Dump the curds into a bowl and add salt. Add enough of the whole milk to form the consistency wanted, and the cottage cheese is ready to serve.

Mushroom and Cheese Omelet

1 tablespoon butter
½ cup mushrooms
¼ cup chopped onion
2 eggs
2 tablespoons milk or water
Grated cheddar cheese

Melt the butter in a skillet over medium heat. Lightly brown the mushrooms and the onion in the butter. Beat the eggs in milk or water. Add the egg mixture to the mushrooms and onions. As the omelet cooks on the underside, lift up with a spatula to allow the uncooked top portions to run underneath. When eggs are almost cooked through, turn off the heat and cut omelet in half or quarters. Sprinkle the omelet with the grated cheese and serve when cheese is melted.

Butter Cookies

1 cup butter, softened
1 cup powdered sugar
1 egg, beaten
1 teaspoon vanilla
2 cups flour
1 teaspoon baking soda
1 teaspoon cream of tartar
½ cup chopped nuts

Preheat oven to 350 degrees. Beat butter and sugar in a large bowl until creamy. Add beaten egg and vanilla. In a separate bowl, mix dry ingredients. Add to sugar mixture. Add nuts last. Form into small balls on ungreased cookie sheets and flatten with fork. Bake until set, 8 to 10 minutes.

CHAPTER 10

BUTCHERING TIME

As was true of most of our neighbors, in addition to milking cows and rais-ing chickens, we also raised pigs. The number during any given year varied, from twenty or so to as many as one hundred during the war years, when the price for pork was higher. In most years we had a few sows, one boar, and several litters of little pigs we grew out for market and for our own use.

Some distance from the other buildings (pigs can be smelly), a hog house provided shelter for the pigs during all seasons of the year. It was in a little fenced pasture, where the pigs could root in the dirt, eat grass, and exercise. If a sow farrowed in early spring, when it was still well below freezing at night, Pa would bring the little pigs into the house in a box and place them behind the kitchen stove to keep them warm.

We fed the pigs ground feed (corn and oats)—the same as we fed our dairy cows, but mixed with water in five-gallon pails. One of my chores when I was about twelve was to mix the feed with water and carry the "slop" to the pigpen, where I poured it into a wooden trough. To fatten the pigs for market and for butchering, we fed them ripe ear corn for several weeks in the fall. When I got home from school I would hitch the team to a wagon, drive out to the cornfield, snap ripe ears off the cornstalks, and toss them into the wagon. Back at the pig yard I'd throw the ears on the ground for the pigs to eat. A pig born in April, properly fed, can reach about two hundred pounds by butchering time.

Among the many farm tasks in November, butchering a hog ranked near the top in importance. Pa and our nearest neighbor, Bill Miller, helped each other with the job, which brought a mixture of excitement, strange smells, and hard work for all of us. Killing the hog, although abhorred by our city cousins, was the easy part. After the killing, removing the coarse hair from the carcass was both dangerous and difficult, for it required immersing the carcass in a fifty-five-gallon metal barrel containing boiling water, rapidly retrieving it, and then scraping off the hair with a hog scraper. When Pa removed the entrails, it was my job to have a big dishpan handy into which he placed the hog's liver and heart. The head remained on the carcass.

HEADCHEESE

Let's begin by saying that other than its name, headcheese has nothing in common with cheese. Headcheese is made from the meat found on a pig's head, including the tongue and the snout. (The eyes and brains are not used.)

Headcheese is a very practical food, allowing one to use as much as possible from a butchered hog—or, as some old-time farmers said, "everything but the squeal." Ma placed the entire hog's head, plus a couple of pork hocks, in a big cooking pot filled with water. The hocks contributed gelatin, which was necessary to hold the headcheese together. Ma allowed the pot to simmer on the woodstove for most of a day, long enough that the meat could readily be removed from the head.

When the meat was tender, Ma removed the head from the pot, saving the water. She pulled off the skin and discarded it. Then she removed every morsel of meat, put it all in a big bowl, and covered it with cooking water. While the meat was cooling, she strained the remaining water from the pot and set that aside to cool as well. Pa tossed the picked-clean-of-meat pig head out in the woods for the wild critters to enjoy.

After the cooking water was cooled, Ma removed the fat that had risen to the top and then brought the water to a boil, reducing it by about one half. She added a little salt to taste. She put the meat into a loaf pan, covered it with the reduced cooking water, and then put the pan in a cool place in the kitchen to set. Once the headcheese was set, she would slice it and serve it with bread.

Although the process sounds arduous and even a bit gruesome, everyone in our family enjoyed headcheese.

The hog carcass hung cooling in the shed overnight. The next day Pa used a meat saw to cut off the head and to slice the carcass in half lengthwise. We carried the head and the halves into the kitchen and put them on the kitchen table. All day long, Ma and Pa, with sharp butcher knives and the meat saw, cut up the meat. First they cut out the hams. Then they removed the two bacon sides, one from each half. Pa had the hams and bacon sides smoked at a butcher shop in Wautoma, and they would hang in the cellar all winter without spoiling.

Pork chops came next. Ma set several aside for meals during the next few days. The remainder she placed in a five-gallon crock, stacked between layers of melted lard, where they would remain for a couple of months or until we had eaten all of them. Ma and Pa cut the rest of the meat into small hunks for canning, except for the head meat (jowls, tongue, snout), which Ma made into headcheese. She cut the fat into small cubes and began rendering it by melting the cubes in a kettle on the woodstove. Once the fat had melted, she separated it from the cracklings, strained it through a cheesecloth, and put it into jars or layered it in a crock with pork chops. If done properly, the rendered lard was as white as snow. Ma used it in all of her baking.

Ma had many pork recipes, and we enjoyed pork dishes two or three times a week during the winter. I especially liked her baked pork chops, as well as thick slices of smoked ham heated in a skillet on the woodstove. And fried bacon, and then eggs fried in the bacon grease. Headcheese was mighty tasty as well, once you got past the source of the meat.

Baked Pork Chops and Gravy

1 pork chop per person
Salt and pepper
1 tablespoon flour
½ cup milk

Preheat oven to 300 degrees. Sprinkle the chops with salt and pepper to taste. Put in a 9 x 13-inch pan. Bake uncovered for about an hour. Remove the chops from the pan. Scrape the drippings from the pan into a skillet on top of the stove. Sprinkle the flour into the drippings. Using a whisk to stir, slowly add the milk to the flour mixture. Cook until smooth. Gravy can be served on the side or poured over the chops.

Pork Cake from Doris

This is exactly how Eleanor printed it on her recipe card. "Makes for cakes" means four cakes.

1 lb. pork chopped fine, salt or fresh
2 cups of boiling water pour over pork
2 cups sugar
1 cup molasses
4 or 5 cups of flour
1 teaspoon soda
1 teaspoon cinnamon and nutmeg
½ teaspoon ginger
1 lb. dates
2 lbs. raisins
2 eggs the last thing

I put in one medium can of maraschino cherries, both cherries and juice

Makes for cakes, bake in slow oven for 1 hr.

Honey-Glazed Ham

10- to 12-pound fully cooked ham
2 cups apple cider
1 teaspoon whole cloves
¾ teaspoon whole allspice
3 cinnamon sticks
1 cup honey, divided
Paprika

Preheat oven to 325 degrees. Place ham, fat side up, on a rack in a shallow baking pan. Insert meat thermometer into the center of the ham so it does not touch the bone. Combine apple cider, cloves, allspice, and cinnamon sticks in a saucepan. Bring to a boil, then cover and boil for 5 minutes. Remove from heat and brush a little of this mixture over the ham.

Cover ham and bake 1½ to 2 hours, basting every 15 minutes with the spiced apple cider mixture. Drizzle ½ cup honey over the ham. Bake 30 minutes longer. Remove from the oven and drizzle on the remaining ½ cup honey. Bake uncovered for 30 more minutes. The internal temperature on the thermometer should be 160 degrees. Remove from oven and let rest for 30 minutes. Score the ham and sprinkle with paprika.

Sliced Smoked Ham with Brown Sugar

Rub a thick slice of ham with 2 tablespoons flour and 2 tablespoons brown sugar and place in a baking dish. Add juice from one small can of crushed pineapple. Bake at 350 degrees for 1 hour.

Ham Slice Meal

Cut fully cooked ham in 1-inch-thick slices. This will prevent curling when they bake. Place ham slices in an ungreased baking dish. Bake uncovered at 325 degrees for 30 minutes.

For another option, place one ham slice in a baking pan. Spread 1½ cups prepared mincemeat over ham; cover with second ham slice. Pour ½ cup pineapple juice over the top. Bake at 325 degrees, basting with the juice frequently. You can use the liquid in the pan to make a spicy gravy.

Smoked Pork Hocks

4 pounds smoked pork hocks (about 4)
4 cups water
1 sliced onion
½ teaspoon marjoram leaves
4 cups sauerkraut, drained
½ teaspoon celery seed
1 apple, sliced

Heat the pork hocks, water, onion, and marjoram to boiling in a pot on top of the stove. Reduce the heat, cover, and simmer for 1½ hours. Drain the liquid from the pot, saving 1 cup of liquid.

Stir the 1 cup of saved liquid, sauerkraut, and celery seed into the pork hocks in the pot. Cover and simmer 15 minutes. Add the apple slices and simmer 15 minutes longer.

CATTLE FAIR

Popular in the 1930s through the 1950s, cattle fairs resembled today's farmers' markets, but with even more to offer. Many cities and small towns had a downtown section set aside for these events. The fairs operated from spring through fall, and we visited two cattle fairs a few times each year, one in Stevens Point and one in Princeton, usually in the fall.

At the cattle fair we could buy and sell everything from freshly harvested vegetables to live chickens, ducks, geese, turkeys, and pigs, including feeder pigs, which weighed about forty pounds and had recently been weaned from their mothers. Pa sold our excess feeder pigs at the cattle fairs.

On a fall Saturday, Pa and I headed off to the cattle fair in Stevens Point in our 1936 Plymouth. We arrived around ten thirty and immediately saw people everywhere: the sellers, with their displays all around the market square, and the buyers, walking from display to display and talking with each other and with the farmers who had things to sell. Live turkeys, ducks, pigs, and geese sounded like an animal orchestra. I loved the exotic mixture of sights, sounds, and smells.

Pa might have been selling a dozen broilers that we had butchered the previous day, or a half-dozen feeder pigs, or a couple bushels of recently dug potatoes. Whatever we took to the fair we hauled in the back of the old Plymouth, which had had its back seat removed. Pa usually bought something as well, sometimes a live duck for our Thanksgiving dinner. He passed by the displays of squash, pumpkins, potatoes, late sweet corn, rutabagas, and popcorn, all of which we grew at home.

At noon we sat under a tree and ate the lunch that Ma had packed for us: bologna sandwiches on homemade bread, an apple and a couple of oatmeal cookies for each of us, and a thermos of coffee for Pa. We talked about all that we had seen and about the prices farmers were getting for their produce. After lunch and a brief rest, we walked around, occasionally meeting a farmer Pa knew and sharing a story or two. Around three o'clock, Pa fetched his watch from the pocket in his bib overalls, looked at it, stuffed it back in the pocket, and said, "Time for us to go." With a live duck in a burlap bag in the back of the Plymouth, we headed back to the farm, arriving in plenty of time for the afternoon chores.

CHAPTER 11

HUNTING FOR GAME

To supplement our meat supply (mainly chicken and pork, and a little beef), especially in the late fall and early winter, we depended on wild meat, which included squirrels, rabbits, Canada geese, and ruffed grouse from our wood-lot, and, in most years, a deer that Pa shot in Adams County. By the time my brothers and I were ten years old, each of us was quite comfortable shooting a rifle and bringing home a squirrel or a cottontail rabbit for the table. Pa taught us how to safely use his old Stevens .22 rifle and how to bring down a squirrel or rabbit with one shot—the killing must be humane, he insisted. By the time I was twelve, I had saved up enough money to buy my own .22 rifle, a Remington Model 512A. Pa also taught us how to skin

Herman Apps and Bill Miller, back from deer hunting

and clean rabbits and squirrels, so when we brought them into the house they were ready for Ma to prepare for the table.

For squirrels, Pa taught us how to make slits along the back legs and down the belly and then, putting a foot on the squirrel's tail, pull on the back legs to remove the skin in one piece. Properly done, we could skin a squirrel in a couple of minutes. We saved the tails, for which we received ten cents apiece, I believe paid by the county. The squirrel-tail hair was used to make flies for fly-fishing. With fur removed, we took out the entrails and tossed them in the woods, and the squirrel was ready for the pan.

Rabbits are easier to skin than squirrels. Simply cut around each leg just above the leg joint, and then on each leg make a cut from the previous one to the backside of the carcass. Pull the hide from the carcass starting where you made the first cuts. When the hide is mostly removed, cut the head from the carcass. Remove the entrails and carefully wash the meat before cutting it into pieces. We all preferred fried rabbit over fried squirrel. As I remember, rabbit didn't have as much "wild" or gamy taste as squirrel. Ma cooked all the hunted meat with plenty of onions to help quiet the wild flavor.

Starting in late November, we ate venison several times a week, if Pa was successful in bagging a deer. Pa always skinned the deer himself, and then Ma helped him cut the meat into pieces—steaks and chops—and process some of the venison into ground meat. In addition to fried venison steak, which we all enjoyed, Ma used venison to make meat loaf and meatballs. We took some of the meat to a meat market and had it made into smoked venison sausage; if stored in a cool place, it kept for several months.

Pa took the deer hides to a tannery in Berlin, where they tanned the hides and made them into buckskin gloves for all of us. They were soft and comfortable and wore like iron. We nailed the deer antlers to the end of the pump house, a reminder of Pa's hunting success.

A few ruffed grouse (we called them partridges) found a home in our woodlot, but they were difficult to shoot. They flew up with an explosion of noise that usually surprised me so much that the bird was gone before I could bring the gun to my shoulder. But one day I was lucky.

My cousin Burton, who lived in Milwaukee and was a few years older than me, stopped by the farm one Saturday with the intention of hunting grouse. He had a fancy new 12-gauge shotgun, and he asked me if I would go along and help him find some birds. I quickly agreed and grabbed my .22

*Brother Donald
after a successful
goose hunt*

rifle—which is not the gun of choice for grouse hunting. If you want any chance of bagging a ruffed grouse you need a shotgun, not a .22 rifle.

I said I would walk through the woods and scare up a ruffed grouse so he could get a shot. As I stood at the edge of the woods, waiting for Cousin Burt to get into position, a ruffed grouse landed not fifty feet from where I was standing. I lifted up my .22 and shot it in the head, killing it instantly. I picked up the bird and started my walk through the woods. In a few minutes, I met up with my cousin. When he saw the grouse I was carrying, he said, "You shot that?"

"I did," I said.

"You shot that grouse on the fly through the head with a .22 rifle," he stated, somewhat incredulous.

I didn't answer, leaving him to think whatever he wanted about my skills with a .22 rifle.

One way to prepare grouse for the table is to place the carcass breast up on the ground. Step on each wing near the body, grab the bird's feet, and pull upward. This will leave you with breast meat with the wings attached (most of the meat on a grouse is in the breast). Remove the wings, wash the breast meat, and it is ready for the oven.

Fried Squirrel

Clean the dressed squirrel with a damp cloth and cut into pieces for serving. Disjoint legs at body and split down the center of the back through the breast. Cut each half into two pieces. Dip pieces into flour seasoned with salt and pepper. Add some chopped onion. Brown in hot fat in a skillet. Reduce heat and cook until tender, about 1 hour. (If the squirrel is old, add a small amount of hot water to the pan. Cover tightly and cook over low heat for 1½ hours until tender.)

Baked Rabbit

 1 rabbit, cleaned and cut into pieces
 1¾ teaspoons salt
 1 tablespoon ground black pepper
 ¼ cup vegetable oil
 1 onion, chopped
 1 cup water
 ¾ cup ketchup
 1½ tablespoons Worcestershire sauce
 4 teaspoons sugar

Preheat oven to 350 degrees. Season rabbit pieces with salt and pepper. Heat vegetable oil in a large frying pan over medium-high heat. Add rabbit pieces and brown on all sides. Place in a 9 x 13-inch baking pan.

In a medium bowl, combine the onion, water, ketchup, Worcestershire sauce, and sugar. Pour over the browned pieces of rabbit. Bake, uncovered, for 1½ hours. Baste frequently.

Marinade for Roast Venison

1 onion, or more if desired

1 carrot

1 rib celery

2 tablespoons fat or vegetable oil

A bouquet of parsley, thyme, bay leaf, and a few whole cloves tied
together in cheesecloth

1 cup vinegar

3- to 4-pound venison roast

3 strips salt pork

Garlic

Chop the onion, carrot, and celery. In a skillet, cook in hot fat or oil with
the spice bouquet for 1 to 2 minutes. Add the vinegar and bring to a boil.
Turn down the heat and simmer for 20 minutes. Strain and then cool.
Put the venison in a glass, not metal, container. Pour the marinade over
the venison. Refrigerate for 24 hours.

Preheat oven to 350 degrees. Remove meat from marinade and rub it
well with salt pork and a few pieces of garlic. Roast on a rack in a shallow
pan for 30 minutes per pound of meat. Baste frequently while roasting.

Fried Venison and Pork Patties

1 pound venison
1 pound pork sausage
1 teaspoon salt
¼ teaspoon pepper
¼ teaspoon thyme
Flour
2 tablespoons butter or lard

Grind together the venison and the pork. Mix in the seasonings. Flour your hands and form the meat into patties. Heat the fat in a skillet and fry the patties on low heat, about 15 minutes on each side or until they are cooked through. Place on a paper towel to absorb fat when done.

Venison Stew

2 pounds boneless venison, cut into cubes
2 tablespoons oil
4¼ cups water, divided
½ cup tomato juice
3–4 small onions, cut in pieces
2 ribs celery, chopped
2 bay leaves
3 teaspoons salt
½ teaspoon pepper
6 potatoes, peeled and cubed
6 carrots, peeled and chopped
1 large rutabaga, peeled and cubed
1 cup peas, frozen or fresh
1–2 tablespoons cornstarch, if needed

In a large pot, brown the meat in oil. Add 4 cups water and loosen any of the meat from the bottom of the pot. Add the tomato juice, onions, celery, bay leaves, salt, and pepper. Bring to a boil. Reduce the heat, cover, and simmer for 2 hours. Add the potatoes, carrots, and rutabaga. Cover and cook until the vegetables are soft and tender, about 1 hour. Stir in the peas and cook for 15 minutes. If needed for thickening, combine the remaining ¼ cup water and cornstarch and add to the soup.

Baked Ruffed Grouse or Partridge

1 ruffed grouse or partridge, cleaned
Flour
Salt pork or bacon fat
½ bunch carrots, sliced
1 onion, sliced
Thyme
1 bay leaf
Salt
Pepper
Paprika
Meat stock or bouillon cubes if necessary for gravy

Preheat oven to 350 degrees. Cut the cleaned bird into pieces and split the breast. Lightly dust the meat with flour. Sauté in a deep pan in salt pork or bacon fat with carrots and onion. When nicely browned, add the thyme, bay leaf, salt, pepper, and paprika and cover with water. Bake until the meat is tender, 40 minutes to 1½ hours. It should be cooked through, but if it is the least bit overdone, the meat will be dry. As soon as the meat is done, take it out and keep warm. Taste the gravy in the pan. If the flavor is right, add water only. If the gravy tastes flat, add meat stock, salt, or bouillon cubes.

CHAPTER 12

FISHING IN SUMMER AND WINTER

After a rainy night in June or July, and the foggy, drizzly morning that often followed, Pa might forgo his usual rainy-day work, such as fixing fence or cleaning out the calf pen, and suggest we go fishing. Farm work kept us so busy in summer that we fished only a few times during those months. But we loved fishing, and we always had our cane fishing poles at the ready, tucked up under the eaves of the corncrib where they would be out of the weather but retrievable with the first hint that fishing was a possibility. The poles, purchased at Hotz's Hardware in Wild Rose, were twelve to fourteen feet long, long enough so we could toss a line out into the lake from shore, but not so long that we tangled one another when we fished from a boat. We used thick green fishing line, all wrapped around the pole, as we had no fancy fishing reels. Our rule of thumb was to have the line half again as long as your pole—thus a twelve-foot pole had eighteen feet of line. Big red-and-white bobbers were fastened to the line, but only tentatively, as we'd have to adjust them according to the depth of the water. We each had a hook (also from Hotz's, where they were sold in bulk) tied to our line and a couple of extras in case a monster fish managed to tear a hook loose. (That never happened in my experience.)

Once we had retrieved our poles and tied them onto the roof of the 1936 Plymouth, we found an empty pork and beans can, grabbed a six-tine fork from the barn, and went digging in a moist spot behind the chicken house where earthworms were usually in abundance, unless it happened to be a drier than average year. We counted the worms as we found them, usually declaring that three or four dozen were enough.

Then we were off to Norwegian Lake, talking on the way about whether the fish would be biting and what we might catch. Arriving at the lake, we stopped at the Thompson farm, which had boats for rent—leaky wooden boats, one dollar for all day.

Pa took the oars and rowed us to a place where he said the bluegills would be biting. Not long after we dropped the anchor, baited our hooks, and flung our lines into the water, sure enough, the bluegills began biting. After a couple of hours, we had twenty-five or so hand-sized fish, some larger and some smaller, in the five-gallon pail that we had brought along. One of us kept an eye on the leaky boat, and if necessary did a little bailing to keep our feet from getting wetter than they already were. When the fish are biting, who pays much attention to whether the boat's filling with water?

Herman fishing from a boat, 1968

Back home, with our fishing poles tucked up under the corncrib eaves and the extra worms dumped on the ground behind the chicken house, we cleaned our catch, looking forward to a fish fry that evening.

PREPARING PAN FISH FOR COOKING

For bluegills, sunfish, and perch, the commonly caught pan fish, we removed the scales, cut off the heads, and removed the entrails, in that order. We'd do the scaling outside, as the scales tend to fly in every direction. (For those concerned about bones, take hold of the back of the fish and spread it open, which reveals the back and side bones. Most bones can be removed in one motion.) Then we'd wash the fish in cold water, and it was ready for the cast-iron skillet. Pa said there was nothing sweeter than eating pan-fried bluegills caught in cold water and prepared within a few hours.

This ice fishing group in 1956 included (left to right) Herman Apps, Frank Kolka, Donald Apps, Darrel Apps, and David Kolka.

Summer fishing was more fun than a necessity. But Pa took ice fishing more seriously, as winter-caught fish were a major supplement to our meat supply. Not that ice fishing wasn't fun, as long as you dressed for it, had a more than average amount of patience, didn't mind sitting by a smoky campfire, and could put up with nonstop storytelling. All of the above were integral parts of ice fishing when I was a kid.

Mount Morris was our favorite lake for ice fishing. It was relatively shallow, with a goodly population of northern pike along with bluegills, sunfish, bass, and perch, and it featured a wooded area on the west side where we could build a campfire, get out of the wind, and still see our tip-ups. Occasionally Pa would bring along his pan-fishing equipment with the idea of snagging a few bluegills, but this was clearly a cold weather project as the fisherman hunched over a little hole in the ice, far from the warm campfire, hoping a bluegill might bite. (Mostly they didn't.) What we really wanted were northern pike. The bag limit was five pike per person per day. We usually did not catch our limit, for that would mean twenty fish for me, Pa, and my brothers. But we did sometimes return home with ten pike, ranging from two or three pounds to five pounds or more.

We fished most days during Christmas break, and on winter weekends when school was in session. Ma packed a lunch for us, and we were off to the lake. We usually arrived at the lake by ten or so, after the barn chores were finished. At our fishing spot, we were often greeted by the Kolka boys, Jim and Dave, who liked ice fishing. My uncle Wilbur was usually there too, along with the Nelsons and the Keenlances.

At noon we found a forked stick in the brush along the shore. Then we opened our lunch pails, dug out our sandwiches, and toasted them over our smoky campfire. The sandwiches were often cheese, which would melt just a bit, or perhaps bologna, which tasted so much better when it was roasted a bit over the fire. Crisp apples and Ma's homemade chocolate chip cookies rounded out the noon meal.

Winter days are short, so by four in the afternoon it was already becoming dark as we headed for the car with our day's catch. Back home, we cleaned the fish. The common way of preparing northern pike for cooking is to filet them, meaning you cut strips of the meat away from the backbone and skin the fish before cooking it, but Pa did not believe in fileting fish—he said it wasted too much meat. Instead we scaled them (leaving on the skin), cut off the heads and removed the entrails, and then cut the fish into pieces about two inches thick. (To those who might complain about bones left in the fish, Pa had no answer other than telling them to eat around the bones.) Ma prepared pike in a variety of ways, including frying and baking. Pa also pickled northern pike to preserve it—a process that caused the unwelcome bones to disintegrate.

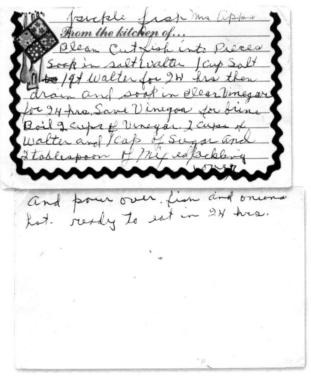

Basic Fried Fish

Dip fish in milk. Sprinkle with salt, pepper, and paprika. Then roll in flour, cornmeal, cracker crumbs, or bread crumbs to coat. Heat oil or melted shortening in a pan. Add fish quickly and cook over medium heat until fish is crisp and golden on the underside. Gently turn with a spatula and cook until the fish flakes easily with a fork. Total cooking time is about 8 minutes. Drain fish on paper towels and transfer to a platter. Keep warm until ready to serve.

Homemade Fish Sauce

1 cup mayonnaise
1 tablespoon sweet pickle relish
1 tablespoon minced onion
1–2 tablespoons lemon juice
Salt and pepper
Garlic pepper sauce or Tabasco sauce (optional)

Mix the mayonnaise, pickle relish, and minced onion in a bowl. Stir in the lemon juice. Season to taste with salt and pepper. Tastes better if you refrigerate for an hour before serving. For a spicy sauce, add garlic pepper sauce or Tabasco sauce to taste and use less pickle relish.

Beer Batter Fried Fish

1 cup flour
2 teaspoons garlic powder
½ teaspoon salt
⅛ teaspoon pepper
1 egg, beaten
1½ cups beer
2 cups crushed cornflake cereal or bread crumbs
1 pound fish fillets, cleaned and ready to fry
Oil for frying

Set up the fish-coating stations like this:
Mix together the flour, garlic powder, salt, and pepper in one bowl.
Mix together the beaten egg and beer in another bowl.
Have the crushed cornflakes or bread crumbs ready on a plate.

When everything is ready, prepare each fillet, keeping one hand "dry" for the flour bowl and crumbs plate and one hand "wet" for dipping into the egg and beer. Place the fillet in the flour and lightly dust with flour mixture. Place fish in egg-and-beer bowl and turn to coat thoroughly. Dip the egg-coated fish into the crumbs and thoroughly coat all sides.

Heat the oil in a large, deep skillet. Fry the fish until golden brown and the fish flakes easily with a fork. Place fried fish on layers of paper towels while waiting to serve.

Baked Fish

4 to 6 freshwater fish
Salt and pepper
2 tablespoons lemon juice
¼ cup butter, melted

Clean the fish and rinse well in cold water. Season with salt and pepper. Mix the lemon juice and melted butter. Put the fish in a greased pan and pour the butter and lemon juice over the fish. Bake at 350 degrees until the fish flakes easily with a fork, about 30 minutes.

Baked Northern Pike

1 large onion, chopped
Butter
2 northern pike, cut in 2-inch-thick slices
1 can (16 ounces) seasoned stewed tomatoes
Salt and pepper
1 teaspoon basil leaves

Preheat oven to 350 degrees. In a pan, sauté the onions in butter. Place the pike slices in a greased baking pan. Season to taste with salt and pepper. Place lightly cooked onions on the fish. Spoon the tomatoes over the fish slices. Sprinkle the basil over the fish. Bake until the fish flakes easily, about an hour depending on the thickness of the fish.

Baked Fish with Bacon

4–5 slices bacon, uncooked
2 pounds fish fillets, cleaned
½ cup condensed tomato soup or homemade tomato sauce
2 medium onions, sliced
Salt and pepper
Lemon slices

Preheat oven to 350 degrees. Place 2 slices of bacon in a greased baking dish. Place fish on top of the bacon. Cover with remaining bacon. Mix the tomato soup with enough water to make a sauce, or use tomato sauce. Add the sliced onions and salt and pepper to taste to the sauce. Pour carefully over the fish. Place lemon slices on the fish. Bake until the fish flakes easily with a fork, about 30 minutes. Check the dish during baking to be sure there is liquid in the bottom and add water if necessary. To serve, place fish on a platter with bacon and sauce from the pan.

Pickled Fish

These are the directions as they were written on Eleanor's recipe card:

Clean fish. Cut into pieces. Soak in salt water, 1 cup of salt in 1 quart of water, for 24 hours.

Drain the fish and rinse. Soak in clear vinegar for 24 hours. Save the vinegar for brine.

Boil 9 cups of vinegar, 2 cups of water and 1 cup of sugar and 2 tablespoons of pickling spice.

Pour this over fish and pieces of onions. Ready to eat in 24 hours.

CHAPTER 13

MA'S KITCHEN GARDEN

In addition to supervising the chicken flock, Ma oversaw our big vegetable garden, which was located a couple hundred yards north of our farmhouse, tucked up against the woodlot to the north. She decided what to plant and where to plant it, when to hoe and when to harvest. My dad, brothers, and I helped with all aspects of gardening. Pa plowed and smoothed the plot with the team, marked it with a two-row hand-pulled marker, and later tilled it with a one-horse cultivator. We all helped with planting and the never-ending hoeing and weeding, and we all helped with harvesting as well, beginning with the first lettuce and radishes in spring and ending with the pumpkins and squash before the first frost in fall. We depended on the garden for all of our vegetables: lettuce, peas, green beans, navy beans, sweet corn, rutabagas, beets, carrots, cabbage, onions, tomatoes, popcorn, squash, and pumpkins. And Ma grew watermelons too, which we all enjoyed eating on hot, dusty summer days.

In January Ma ordered seeds from one of several seed catalogs we received in the mail. I knew that on those cold, dark, and snowy days, just paging through the seed catalog cheered my mother. I could tell because she was usually smiling as she turned the pages; she smiled the most broadly when she came to the pages of red, ripe tomatoes.

On March 17, Saint Patrick's Day, she planted her tomato seeds in flowerpots filled with garden soil that she had saved from the previous fall. She said that because we celebrated the color green on Saint Patrick's Day, it was a good day for starting garden seeds, such as tomatoes and cabbage.

We began planting the garden in late April: lettuce, onion sets (which Ma bought at the co-op store in Wild Rose), radishes, and carrots. The tomato plants would wait in the kitchen window until the day in late May when Ma figured there would be no more frosty nights. Around each tomato plant that Ma set out in the garden, she placed an old tin can with the top and bottom cut out. Some of those old cans were more than a little rusty after years of use, but they served their purpose, helping to support the little plants, providing some protection from frost, and keeping away cutworms, which would cut off the entire plant.

By late June, Ma's pea crop was ready for picking and processing. Ma kept an eagle eye on the crop, making sure that the peas had reached just the right maturity. When she had determined the proper harvest time, she announced at the breakfast table that the peas were ready and she needed help shucking. Ma did most of the pea picking; she wanted to make sure that the pea pods were filled out just right and the immature pods were left behind. Soon she appeared with a big wash pan heaped full of plump pods and set it down under the elm tree in front of the house. I don't remember how it was decided which of the three brothers got to help shuck peas and which got to continue hoeing potatoes—maybe we took turns. As boring as shucking peas was, it was a lot easier than hoeing, no question about that. Besides, when you shucked peas you got to sit in the shade. Not much shade in the middle of a potato patch.

RHUBARB AND ASPARAGUS

In addition to her garden, Ma maintained a row of rhubarb in front of the pump house and two long rows of asparagus alongside the barnyard fence. We knew that spring had arrived when Ma said the rhubarb was ready for pulling. She made two things from fresh rhubarb: one we liked, and the other we detested. Her rhubarb pie was a special treat, especially after a long winter with no pie. But her rhubarb sauce was awful. And even though my brothers and I didn't like its tart taste, Pa insisted that we eat it, telling us that "rhubarb sauce cleanses the body after a long winter."

Ma watched the asparagus plants carefully, cutting them just when the new stalks were thick and tall, but not so tall that the stalks had become stringy. We all liked her way of preparing fresh asparagus.

As the oldest kid in our family, I didn't have much time to talk with Ma. I was doing either barn chores or field work with Pa. Shucking peas was a special time for the two of us to be together, sitting with the huge pile of peas on a little table in front of us and a smaller pan on each of our laps. Ma had taught us when we were little tykes how to squeeze a pea pod so the fat, green peas popped out and dropped into the pan.

After I'd done about the fiftieth pea pod, the novelty of the task wore mighty thin. But just when I began feeling sorry for myself and wishing I was out hoeing potatoes with Pa, Ma would say something that took my mind completely off pea pods. She might ask me a question about what I'd like to do after high school. Or talk about times she remembered shucking peas with her own mother. Or tell me about the German school she had attended, where no one was allowed to speak or write English. Before I knew it, the pan of pea pods was empty and each of our basins was heaped with wonderful fresh peas that we would eat nearly every day, and that Ma would can in Mason jars and store in the cellar.

By late June the tomatoes had grown well above their tin can shelters, so Ma removed the cans and stored them away for another season. Using wooden stakes that we had cut from our woodlot, we stuck a stake in the ground near each tomato plant and tied the tomato stalk to the stake with binder twine.

Then we waited for the first tomato blossoms to appear, followed by the little green immature tomatoes, and then, finally, a ripe red one. Preparing tomatoes for the table was easy. Ma simply sliced them, piled the slices on a plate, sprinkled them with salt and pepper, and we dove in, adding several slices of fresh tomatoes to our dinner plates. Some people sprinkled a little sugar on their tomatoes, but Pa said that spoiled their taste. "A little pepper," he said, "makes them taste better than they already do." When tomatoes were in season, usually from August until the first frost, we ate tomatoes at least once a day, sometimes twice.

Green beans were ready to eat in July. Ma had a special way with beans, and we enjoyed them a couple times a week when they were in season. By late July the first sweet corn was ready, and how wonderful it was, slathered with butter and sprinkled with salt. Then came the first little beets, cooked, buttered, and sliced on our plates, and the first red potatoes—how good they tasted, dug in the morning and eaten at noon. It seemed each summer week another

GROWING POPCORN

Ma always grew a row of popcorn in her garden. The plants were shorter than sweet corn, as were the ears, which we allowed to ripen and dry on the stalks. Popcorn was one of the last things we harvested from the garden, generally after the squash and pumpkins and usually after a frost, which killed the plant and allowed for further drying. After we harvested the ears of popcorn, we shelled the kernels from the cobs and stored the kernels in glass jars. The jars kept the popcorn safe from mice (as hard as Ma tried to keep mice out of the house, she never quite succeeded) and prevented the kernels from drying too much. It is the heated moisture inside the popcorn kernel that causes the pop.

vegetable was ready for the table, right up into fall when we begin eating the first squash of the season and Ma made the first pumpkin pie.

The first frost was the signal to harvest horseradish from the clump Ma grew behind the chicken house. We largely ignored the horseradish until then, as it required essentially no care once it was planted. After the frost we dug up the larger roots, leaving the smaller ones behind to produce in another year. Ma washed the roots, and then we all took a turn grinding them in her hand-turned food grinder, releasing an extremely pungent smell that brought tears to our eyes. Ma mixed the ground horseradish with vinegar, which slowed the release of the tear-inducing aroma, and stored the mixture in pint jars. We ate horseradish on pork chops, beef, and ham, and Ma used it to add zip to her meals.

After the fall harvest, we stored the rutabagas, onions, squash, and pumpkins in the cellar under the house; the watermelons we buried in the granary's oat bin, which kept them from freezing. The navy beans, once dried, were stored in gallon jars in the pantry. Ma canned peas, carrots, green beans, tomatoes, and sweet corn, ensuring we'd have vegetables to eat throughout the winter and early spring.

Rhubarb Custard Pie

1 cup cut-up rhubarb pieces
¼ teaspoon baking soda
Boiling water
1 cup sugar
1 tablespoon flour
2 eggs
1 cup milk
1 tablespoon butter, melted
Pastry for a single-crust pie, rolled out

Preheat oven to 350 degrees. In a medium bowl, sprinkle rhubarb pieces with baking soda and cover with boiling water. Let stand until just warm. Drain and squeeze the water out of the rhubarb. Combine with sugar and flour.

In another bowl, beat the eggs and add the milk and melted butter. Line a pie plate with pastry and fill with rhubarb mixture. Pour egg mixture over rhubarb and bake until firm, 45 to 50 minutes.

Rhubarb Sauce

3–4 cups chopped rhubarb
1 cup sugar
⅓ cup water or less

Put rhubarb pieces in a medium cooking pot. The sauce will bubble while cooking, so be sure your pot is big enough. Add the sugar and a bit of water to help the sauce start cooking. Start over a medium heat, and then reduce the heat to a simmer as soon as it begins to bubble or boil. Keep uncovered and stir frequently so the sauce doesn't stick to the pot. Let simmer until the rhubarb cooks down, about 25 minutes. Let cool and then refrigerate.

New Peas with Onions

4 cups fresh shelled peas
1 teaspoon sugar
Pinch of salt
1 cup sliced small green onions
2 tablespoons butter, melted

Put peas in a saucepan with sugar, salt, and enough water to cover and cook until just tender, 5 to 10 minutes. Drain off any unevaporated water. In another pan, cook the onions in boiling water until just tender, about 10 minutes. Drain the onions. Add to the cooked peas and stir together. Add melted butter.

Peas and Cabbage

1½ cups fresh shelled peas
1 head of cabbage, washed and cut up into bite-sized chunks
2 tablespoons butter
Salt and pepper

Cook peas in boiling salted water until tender. Drain off the water. In another pan, cook the cabbage in a small amount of water until tender crisp. Drain the cabbage. Mix the cabbage with the peas and butter; season with salt and pepper to taste.

Fresh Peas and Cheese Salad

Mix together cut-up pieces of fresh lettuce, cubes of cheddar cheese, cubes of cooked ham, and fresh peas. Make a dressing with ½ cup mayonnaise, 2 tablespoons milk, 1 tablespoon sugar, and salt and pepper to taste. Add as much dressing as you like to coat the lettuce and other ingredients.

Spring Asparagus

2 pounds fresh asparagus stalks
⅓ cup butter
⅓ cup water
Salt and pepper

In the garden or in the wild, break off the asparagus stalk as far down as it snaps easily. Wash and scrub with a clean cloth to wipe off dirt or sand. Scrape off scales with a knife.

Lay the stalks on a cutting board and cut into pieces. Make diagonal cuts for a fancier look.

Heat the butter and water together in a skillet until butter is melted. Add asparagus and season with salt and pepper to taste. Cover and cook over high heat for 3 to 5 minutes, stirring occasionally. Asparagus is done when it is tender crisp but not limp.

Fresh Sweet Corn on the Cob

Cook fresh corn as soon as you can after picking. Store in the refrigerator or in a cool place until ready to cook. Husk the corn and remove the silk just before cooking. Place corn in enough cold water to cover. Do not put salt in the water. Add 1 tablespoon sugar to the water. Heat to boiling. Boil uncovered for 2 minutes. Take the pot off the heat and cover. Let stand for 10 minutes before serving.

Cooked Fresh Carrots

Wash the carrots and remove the green carrot tops. Scrape or peel the carrots. Cut into strips or slices. Heat 2 cups of water with 1 teaspoon salt to boiling. Add the carrots. Cook until tender, about 20 minutes. Drain the water from the carrots. Serve with melted butter, salt, and pepper. You can also add fresh snipped parsley, chives, or snipped pieces of green onion. Cooked carrots can also be mashed or creamed.

Cooked Fresh Beets

5 medium beets
6 cups water
1 tablespoon vinegar
1 teaspoon salt

Wash the beets and cut off the tops. Heat the water, vinegar, and salt to boiling. Add the beets. Heat to boiling again and cook until beets are tender, about 40 minutes. Drain the beets and run cold water over them. Remove the skins and the roots (the skins will slip off). Slice the beets and serve.

Harvard Beets

2 tablespoons butter or oleo (margarine)
1 teaspoon cornstarch
¼ cup sugar
¼ cup vinegar
2 tablespoons water
½ teaspoon salt
Dash of pepper
2 cups cubed or sliced cooked beets

Melt the butter or oleo in a saucepan. Add cornstarch and blend. Add sugar, vinegar, water, salt, and pepper. Cook and stir over moderate heat until the mixture is thick and clear. Fold into hot beets and set aside in a warm place to allow flavors to blend, 4 to 5 minutes.

Homemade Horseradish

3 to 4 horseradish roots, tops removed (If you do not grow your
own horseradish, purchase about 2 pounds of the roots, which
will make about 2 cups of grated horseradish. Make sure the
roots are fresh, not limp.)
1 cup vinegar (5% acidity)
½ teaspoon pickling salt
¼ teaspoon powdered ascorbic acid

Wash the roots thoroughly, removing all dirt. With a vegetable peeler,
remove the brown outer skin from the roots. Cut the roots into small cubes
and put through a food grinder. This part of the process releases the
materials that affect the sinuses.

Mix vinegar, salt, and ascorbic acid into the ground horseradish. Adding
the vinegar stops the heat from developing. Put in small jars and store in
the refrigerator. Your prepared horseradish will remain good for about
2 months. After that it begins to turn brown and loses its pungency.

CHAPTER 14

CABBAGE AND SAUERKRAUT

When I was growing up, if you were German (and a lot of us in central Wisconsin were), you knew about cabbage, and you especially knew about sauerkraut. If you didn't like sauerkraut, you got over it, for if you were hungry, especially in the wintertime, you ate sauerkraut.

Along with her tomato seeds, Ma planted cabbage seeds on Saint Patrick's Day. She grew two varieties, an early maturing variety and a late variety. As the seedlings sprouted and grew in a south window of our kitchen, Ma tended them as lovingly as she cared for newly hatched chicks. She set the cabbage plants out in the garden by late April to early May, as cabbage is a cool weather crop and can even survive a light frost. Ma planted them in a row stretching from one end of the garden to the other and then hoed the little plants regularly, replacing the occasional one that died or succumbed to a hungry rabbit.

By the beginning of September, the early cabbage was ready to harvest, the green heads as large as an adult's head, plump and firm. Ma made coleslaw and sometimes prepared boiled cabbage from this early variety.

In October the late cabbage was ready, big, leafy, heavy heads that we chopped off with a big butcher knife, tossed into bushel baskets, and carried to the kitchen where our homemade sauerkraut manufactory had been set up. Making sauerkraut was a family project, with Pa working at the cabbage slicer—he said it was too dangerous for us kids to use; Ma tucking the shredded cabbage into the five-gallon Red Wing crock; one of the twins handing heads of cabbage to Pa and the other, following Ma's directions, sprinkling salt on each layer of shredded cabbage in the crock; and me

Cabbage salad
1 med head Cabbage
1 large onion
1 large pepper sprinkle with Salt
and pepper and mix well
Heat to Boiling
3/4 Cup vinegar
1½ cups Sugar
½ cup Cooking oil
a little Mustard & Celery Seed
Pour boiling hot over Cabbage   (over

mix let stand at least 4 hrs

tamping the cabbage in the crock with a big piece of stovewood. The smell of fresh cabbage filled the room, as we five worked for a couple hours, or until we ran out of cabbage or the crock was full.

By late October we were feasting on sauerkraut at least once a week. Ma had many ways of preparing it: baked sauerkraut, fried sauerkraut, sauerkraut and pork chops, sauerkraut and ham, sauerkraut and pork hocks, sauerkraut cake, and sometimes just a bowl of plain old tart-tasting kraut fresh out of the crock.

HOW TO MAKE SAUERKRAUT

The necessary equipment for making sauerkraut consisted of a cabbage slicer (commonly known as a finger shortener because of what could happen if it was not used properly), a five-gallon Red Wing crock, a clean wooden stick, a kitchen plate that fit snugly within the crock, a piece of cheesecloth, and a clean rock that weighed a couple pounds. Here is the process:

1. Remove the coarse outer leaves from the cabbage and discard.
2. Cut the cabbage head into halves and then into quarters.
3. Slice the cabbage into shreds as long as possible and about ⅟₁₆-inch thick.
4. Place the shredded cabbage in layers in the crock. For every 3 or 4 pounds of shredded cabbage, sprinkle all over with 2½ tablespoons of noniodized salt (coarse pickling salt is best).
5. After every two or three layers, tamp the shredded cabbage with a clean piece of wood—don't use anything metal for tamping.
6. Continue filling the container to within 4 or 5 inches of the top. Position the cheesecloth over the cabbage, lapping it over the edge of the crock. Place the snug-fitting dinner plate on top of the cloth.
7. Put the stone on top of the plate. The salt will draw the juice out of the cabbage and make brine, which will rise to the top. Mold may appear on the top of the brine; remove it daily.
8. Store the fermenting kraut in a well-ventilated place with a temperature of 60 to 65 degrees.
9. In three to five days, remove the cover and look at the sauerkraut. Some spoilage may occur on the top inch or so. Remove it. Rinse clean the cloth covering before replacing it.

The kraut should be ready for eating in four to six weeks. It will keep indefinitely in the crock as long as the top is not exposed to air. The kraut can be removed from the crock and canned, as my mother did, or frozen.

Ring Bologna and Sauerkraut Oven Stew

1 large onion, chopped
⅛ teaspoon garlic powder
1 tablespoon oil
1¾ cups diced tomatoes, undrained
1½ cups (or one 14-ounce can) sauerkraut, undrained
6 small potatoes, peeled and halved
1 teaspoon sugar (optional)
1 pound ring bologna, sliced

Preheat oven to 350 degrees. In a pan, sauté the onion and garlic powder in the oil until tender. Transfer the mixture to a 2-quart baking dish. Add the tomatoes, sauerkraut, potatoes, and sugar. Mix gently. Bake for 30 minutes. Place ring bologna slices on top of the vegetables. Cover and bake until the potatoes are soft, about 20 minutes.

Fried Sauerkraut and Wieners

2–3 tablespoons butter
2 cups sauerkraut, drained
Salt and pepper
4 cooked and cut up wieners or sausages

Melt the butter in a frying pan. Add the drained sauerkraut. Sprinkle with salt and pepper. Sauté until browned. Add the cooked wiener pieces.

Chocolate Sauerkraut Cake

1½ cups sugar
⅔ cup butter, softened
3 eggs
1 teaspoon vanilla
2½ cups flour
½ cup unsweetened cocoa powder
1 teaspoon baking powder
1 teaspoon baking soda
¼ teaspoon salt
1 cup water
⅔ cup rinsed, drained, and chopped sauerkraut

Preheat oven to 350 degrees and grease a 9 x 13-inch pan. Cream sugar and butter together in a large bowl. Add eggs and vanilla. In another bowl, combine flour, cocoa powder, baking powder, baking soda, and salt. Add flour mixture to the sugar and egg mixture, alternating with the water and ending with water. Stir in the sauerkraut. Pour into the pan and bake until a toothpick inserted in the middle comes out clean, about 30 minutes.

Boiled Cabbage

Remove outer leaves of 1 medium-sized head of fresh green cabbage and wash thoroughly. Cut the cabbage into wedges or shred cabbage and remove the inside core. In a big pot, heat 1 cup water and ½ teaspoon salt to boiling. Add the cabbage. Cover and heat again to boiling. Cook until crisp tender. Shredded cabbage will take about 5 minutes. Wedges of cabbage will take twice as long. Drain and serve.

Cabbage Salad

1 medium head of cabbage
1 large onion
1 large bell pepper sprinkled with salt and pepper
¾ cup vinegar
1½ cups sugar
½ cup cooking oil
A little mustard seed and a little celery seed

Cut up cabbage, onion, and pepper and mix well. Combine vinegar, sugar, oil, and seasonings in a saucepan and heat to boiling. When the liquid boils, pour over the cabbage mixture. Mix together. Refrigerate for at least 4 hours before serving.

Coleslaw Dressing

1 cup hot water
1 teaspoon celery seed
1 cup sugar
½ cup salad oil
½ cup cider vinegar
½ cup white vinegar
1 tablespoon salt
Dash of pepper

Pour hot water over the celery seed in a quart jar. Add all the other ingredients. Shake well. This will keep a long time in the refrigerator. Mix dressing with shredded cabbage.

Sweet-and-Sour Cabbage

1 head red or white cabbage
Salt and pepper
2–3 sour apples
2 tablespoons butter
Boiling water
2 tablespoons flour
4 tablespoons brown sugar
2 tablespoons vinegar

Clean and shred the cabbage. Add some salt and pepper to taste. Slice or grate the apples and add to the cabbage. Heat the butter in a frying pan and add the cabbage and apples. Pour some boiling water over them and cook until tender.

When the cabbage and apples are tender, sprinkle them with the flour. Add brown sugar and vinegar and mix together. Cook a little longer and then serve hot.

CHAPTER 15

RUTABAGAS

We learned of Pa's plan in April 1946. He announced at the breakfast table one Saturday morning that he was going to plant three acres of rutabagas on a patch of breaking ground (land that had never been plowed) on the far north end of our woodlot. Pa liked rutabagas, which he called "beggies." He had grown up eating them, and he believed that everyone in the world dearly loved to eat rutabagas as he did. He also knew that rutabagas grown on breaking ground were especially prized because they were free of disease and of worms and other pests that often lingered in plots where garden crops were grown year after year.

My brothers and I helped Pa clear the remaining stumps and low-growing shrubs, and with our newly purchased tractor and a breaking plow we plowed what we had already begun to call the rutabaga patch. Then we planted the entire three acres with rutabagas.

We knew what was coming next. If we had any kind of a crop at all, we'd be peddling rutabagas come fall. Peddling, or selling produce door to door, had become one of Pa's favorite ways of turning a crop into cash with no middleman involved. While the dictionary defines *peddle* as "to sell," my definition of the word was trying to sell something to someone who doesn't want what I am selling. But we'd had some success peddling strawberries and potatoes, and Pa's confidence in the approach to selling our excess fruits and vegetables had reached an all-time high. He was ready for the new challenge.

It turned out to be a great growing year for all of our crops, rutabagas included. In early October, we dug them by hand, using six-tined barn forks, and hauled them to the cellar under the house. We had 365 bushels of those special "breaking-ground rutabagas," as Pa called them.

Once the rutabagas were safely stored in the cellar, I asked Pa if he thought we'd be able to peddle so many rutabagas. (I resisted saying that rutabagas were nothing at all like the juicy red strawberries or the always popular potatoes we'd successfully peddled in the past.) He answered, "People like rutabagas. Once we tell them we have breaking-ground beggies, they'll buy lots of them."

Our first peddling trip to Plainfield proved him wrong. On that day, we stuffed a half dozen bushels of breaking-ground beggies into the back of the Plymouth, hoping to sell at least a half a bushel, maybe even a bushel, to each customer.

I don't think we sold more than a dozen rutabagas—individual rutabagas— that entire day. We returned home with most of them. Pa, ever the optimist, said it was "an off day," and we surely would do better the following Saturday when we traveled to Waupaca. But that day was an off day as well, and when the snow began flying, most of the rutabaga crop still rested in a big bin in the cellar under our farmhouse. By late March of the next year, when the weather began to warm, the rutabagas began rotting and the entire house was filled with the most terrible smell. Rutabagas have a goodly amount of sulfur in them, and when they spoil the smell is a lot like that of rotten eggs.

After a Saturday of hard work carrying the spoiled beggies out of the cellar to the manure spreader and spreading them back on the field from which they came, Pa chose not to repeat his rutabaga misadventure the following year. But although peddling rutabagas had proven disastrous, this did not prevent us from continuing to grow long rows of rutabagas in our garden. Pa still believed that they were tasty and healthful. He never could understand why other people didn't agree with him, but he made sure that his family had plenty of beggies to eat.

Boiled Rutabagas

Wash and peel the rutabagas. Cut in slices or in cubes. Cook in a saucepan in a small amount of boiling salted water until done, 25 to 40 minutes.

Mashed Rutabagas

1 large rutabaga
1 teaspoon salt, plus more to taste
3 potatoes
1 cup heavy cream
½ stick butter

Peel the rutabaga and cut it into cubes. Put the rutabaga in a large saucepan and cover with water. Add salt. Bring to a boil over medium heat. Boil the rutabaga for 40 minutes. Peel the potatoes and cut them into cubes. Add the potatoes to the pan during the last 15 minutes and cook until the potatoes are tender.

Heat the cream in a small saucepan. Drain the rutabagas and potatoes and mash with a potato masher. Add the hot cream and butter and continue mashing until the mixture is the desired consistency. Add salt to taste.

Roasted Rutabaga

1 large rutabaga
3 tablespoons oil
Salt and pepper
½ teaspoon apple cider vinegar
Fresh chopped parsley or dried parsley

Preheat oven to 425 degrees. Peel the rutabaga and cut it into cubes. Mix with the oil, salt, and pepper so all pieces are coated. Place rutabaga on a baking sheet. Roast until tender, about 40 minutes. To serve, toss with vinegar and sprinkle with parsley.

Rutabaga Casserole

4 medium rutabagas
¼ cup milk, warmed
4 carrots, grated
2 tablespoons sugar
2 tablespoons butter, melted

Wash and peel the rutabagas. Cut them into large cubes. Place the cubes in a pan of cold salted water and bring to a boil. When the rutabagas are fork tender, drain the water. Add the warm milk to the cooked rutabagas, a little at time. Add only as much as you need to mash the rutabagas with a potato masher until they are smooth. Add the carrots, sugar, and butter and mix together. Place the rutabaga mixture in a casserole dish. Keep the dish in the oven at a low temperature to keep warm until ready to serve. Cover so that the rutabagas will not dry out.

Rutabaga and Beef Oven Stew

2 pounds beef or round steak, cut into 1½-inch cubes
2 medium onions, chopped or sliced
1 cup chopped celery
4 medium carrots, sliced
1 cup tomato juice or one can (8 ounces) tomatoes
½–1 cup red wine (optional)
½ cup tapioca
1 tablespoon sugar
1 tablespoon salt
½ teaspoon basil
¼ teaspoon black pepper
1 cup chopped mushrooms
1–2 medium potatoes, cut into cubes
1–2 medium rutabagas, cut into cubes

Preheat oven to 350 degrees. Combine beef, onions, celery, carrots, tomato juice, wine (if desired), tapioca, sugar, salt, basil, and pepper in a 2½-quart casserole. Cover and cook for 2½ hours. Mix mushrooms, potatoes, and rutabagas into stew. Cook uncovered for 1 hour longer. Stir occasionally. Add a bit of water if stew is thicker than desired.

Rutabaga and Sausage

1 large rutabaga
Smoked sausage
1 cup diced onion
½–1 cup sliced green pepper
Bacon grease

Wash and peel the rutabaga. Cut it into cubes. Cook in boiling water until soft but not mushy; drain. Cut the sausage into small rounds. Fry the sausage, onion, and pepper strips in a bit of bacon grease until brown and tender. Add the cooked rutabaga and fry until it is all nice and brown.

CHAPTER 16

POTATO COUNTRY

Western Waushara County, where I grew up, has long been potato country. The sandy, well-drained soils of this part of the state are especially well suited to growing this crop. During the Depression years of the 1930s, almost everyone in our neighborhood grew potatoes as a cash crop; we grew twenty to thirty acres every year. We planted seed potatoes with a hand potato planter, following a mark in the soil made with a horse-drawn wooden marker that Pa made. We cultivated the field with a one-horse hand-held cultivator several times during the summer; we also hoed them by hand several times, an onerous back-straining task, especially in May, June, and July, when weeds tried to choke out the potato plants. When other work

The Witt family picking potatoes near Kellner in the early 1900s

was completed and the haying season ended, we hoed potatoes. When it had rained and we couldn't work in the grain field, we hoed potatoes. The job was never done—until fall rolled around and it was time for the potato harvest.

We began digging the potatoes in the last days of September. Different from threshing, silo filling, and corn shredding, digging potatoes required a relatively small crew who worked at it for two weeks or more, as all of the work was done by hand. The entire family was involved, along with one or two neighbors who helped out. The country schools in the area closed for "potato vacation" so all the children in the community were available to help with the harvest.

Digging potatoes worked like this. First, Pa used the team and wagon to scatter wooden one-bushel crates across the field. Next, two men—Pa and a neighbor or a hired man—each with a six-tine barn fork, backed their way across the field, digging up two rows of potatoes as they moved along. I followed, picking up the potatoes and putting them into a five-gallon pail. When the pail was filled, I dumped it into the nearest wooden crate. Pa paid me one penny for each bushel of potatoes I picked.

While we worked, the team rested under a shade tree. A few minutes before noon, the diggers quit digging and I finished picking up and dumping potatoes into crates. Pa fetched the team and wagon, and we loaded the crates and hauled them to the cellar under the house. When those bins were filled, we hauled potatoes to the potato cellar, which was built into a hill just west of the chicken house. When the potatoes were unloaded and the horses watered and fed, we filed into the house for the noon meal.

MENU

POTATO-DIGGING NOON MEAL

Baked sauerkraut and wieners	*Dill pickles*
Mashed potatoes and gravy	*Apple pie*
Baked beans	*Coffee*

As soon as we had fresh potatoes, we began eating them, usually three times a day. We never tired of eating potatoes, especially because Ma had so many ways of fixing them. Pa never wavered in his praise for how good potatoes tasted and for how good they were for growing boys (and everyone else) to eat.

Potato Soup

5 large baking potatoes
½ cup sliced carrots
6 slices bacon
1 cup chopped onion
½ cup chopped celery
2 cups milk
2 cups cream
1½ teaspoons salt
¼ teaspoon pepper
Shredded cheddar cheese, for garnish
Chopped fresh parsley (or dried parsley), for garnish

Wash and peel the potatoes and cut into cubes. Cook the potatoes and sliced carrots in boiling water until tender. Drain.

Cook the bacon until crisp. Drain bacon, reserving the fat, and crumble. Sauté the onion and celery in 2 tablespoons bacon fat.

Combine the cooked vegetables, bacon, milk, cream, salt, and pepper in a saucepan. Simmer for 30 minutes, making sure it doesn't boil. Garnish with cheese and parsley.

German Potato Salad

6 baking potatoes
2 cups water, divided
⅓ cup vinegar
½ cup sugar
3 tablespoons cornstarch
½ pound of bacon, fried, with drippings reserved
1 chopped onion (about ½ cup)
¼ cup chopped celery
¼ cup chopped parsley
Salt and pepper

Wash and peel the potatoes and slice thin. Cook the potatoes in boiling water until crisp tender. Drain.

To make the dressing, place 1½ cups water, vinegar, and sugar in a saucepan. Heat to boiling. Mix the cornstarch with the remaining ½ cup water and add to the saucepan. Boil until the mixture is thick, stirring occasionally. Crumble the bacon and stir bacon pieces and some drippings into the dressing. Pour the dressing over the cooked potatoes and mix. Stir in the onion, celery, and parsley. Season to taste with salt and pepper. Serve warm.

Scalloped Potatoes and Ham

6 medium potatoes
3 cups milk
3 tablespoons butter
2 tablespoons flour
2–3 cups cubed cooked ham
2 tablespoons chopped onion
1 teaspoon salt
¼ teaspoon pepper
½ cup grated cheddar cheese (optional)

Preheat oven to 350 degrees. Wash and peel the potatoes. Slice them very thin.

In a saucepan, stir together the milk, butter, and flour over medium heat until the butter is melted. Remove from the heat.

Put half of the potatoes in a greased casserole dish. Add some of the ham. Pour half of the white sauce over the potatoes and the ham. Add the remaining potatoes, onion, salt, and pepper. Sprinkle in the rest of the ham. Pour the rest of the sauce over the potatoes. Cover and bake for about 1 hour. Uncover, top with cheese, if desired, and continue baking until the top is brown.

Potato Pancakes

6 large potatoes
3 tablespoons flour
1 tablespoon milk
1 teaspoons salt
1 egg, beaten well
¼ cup butter

Wash the potatoes and peel them. Grate them into a bowl. Add the flour, milk, salt, and beaten egg to the grated potatoes. Mix well.

Warm a frying pan and melt the butter. Scoop up some of the potato mixture and form into a pancake. Fry the pancake on one side and then turn it over, cooking until brown, about 4 minutes. Repeat with remaining potato mixture.

CHAPTER 17

MA'S STRAWBERRY PATCH

The first strawberry patch that I remember at our farm was located west of the red pine windbreak, just before you arrived at the night pasture. It was about a half-acre and was fenced so the cows couldn't trample the berries. Ma was in charge of the strawberry patch, and she took the responsibility very seriously. During the strawberry season—from early spring, when the plants needed hoeing, through the picking season, which ended in mid-July or so, depending on the weather—we were in Ma's employ. Even Pa had to put off other pressing farm duties when the strawberries were ripe; it was all hands on deck. Along with her chicken flock, Ma's strawberries represented her own income, money that she used for groceries, Christmas and birthday presents, and occasionally clothes and shoes for my brothers and me.

She grew two varieties: Sparkle, a June berry that took up the majority of the patch, and a few rows of ever-bearing strawberries that ripened in June and offered a smaller crop in fall as well. Ma's strawberry patch was a "pick your own" project, meaning that folks from Wild Rose, Wautoma, and other nearby villages would come out to the farm and pick berries, under Ma's watchful eye. She organized the picking to a T. She constructed markers for each row, and when someone arrived to pick (no children allowed in the patch), she assigned them to a row. And they had to stay on their row until it was picked clean, no matter if the row next to it appeared to have better, more luscious berries. She sold the berries by the quart, and most people picked into the wooden quart berry boxes that Ma supplied for pickers who did not have their own.

STRAWBERRY SANDWICH

During strawberry season, one of my favorite treats was a fresh straw-berry sandwich. It was easy to make, and nothing tasted better after a couple hours of back-breaking strawberry picking.

To make a strawberry sandwich, I started with two pieces of Ma's fresh homemade bread, cut thick. On each piece of bread I spread an ample amount of butter. Then I selected a half dozen of the biggest, red-dest, ripest strawberries I could find. I plucked out the hulls and arranged the berries neatly on one slice of the buttered bread. Then, with a fork, I gently pushed down on each strawberry, until it was mostly flat with the juice oozing out in every direction. When I finished crushing all the strawberries, I sprinkled a little sugar over them, put the second piece of bread in place, and took a big bite. Oh, what a wonderful taste. It was the taste of summer, and who cared if strawberry juice ran down my chin. Even Ma didn't comment—though she was usually the one to remind me when my face was dirty. I'm sure she was remembering strawberry sandwiches from when she was a little girl.

Ma was considerably peeved when pickers heaped up their quart boxes, filling them a quart and a half full or more. She reminded them that a quart meant a quart, and that meant level at the top, or perhaps with a tiny bit of heap. Those who did not abide by her rules—stay on your row, no heaping— were not invited back.

My brothers, Pa, and I picked many quarts of strawberries as well, for our own use and for trading at the Mercantile in Wild Rose. Ma traded crates of strawberries (a crate held sixteen quarts) for groceries. During strawberry season, we'd bring several crates of strawberries to the Mercantile at least twice a week—on free movie night, which was Tuesday, and on our regular Saturday evening trip to town.

Sometimes when the strawberry crop was especially good, Pa and we boys loaded several quarts of strawberries in the back of our 1936 Plymouth and headed toward one of the nearby towns—Plainfield, Wautoma, Pine River, or Waupaca. We stayed away from Wild Rose, because Ma didn't want us to compete with the Mercantile, one of her best customers.

Peddling strawberries worked like this. Pa would send my "cute" twin brothers to knock on a prospective customer's door, each carrying a nicely filled quart of freshly picked strawberries. (To make sure the berries looked especially fresh, Pa always dumped them into a fresh box after the ride in the Plymouth.) I stood a couple steps in back of my brothers. As the eldest, I was expected to have answers at the ready for the customers' questions: "Where are you from? How much are your berries? Are these two cute little guys twins?" It was that last question that usually got my goat, but I smiled and answered, always hoping to sell at least two quarts, maybe even three or four. And we usually did.

Ma saved some strawberries for our family to eat, of course, and eat them we did. We loved them in fresh strawberry pie and sauce, in Ma's homemade jam, and even the deceptively simple sounding strawberry sandwich.

Strawberry Pie

Prepared crust for a 1-crust pie (can substitute a graham
  cracker crust)
4 cups fresh strawberries
1½ cups water
½ cup sugar
2 tablespoons cornstarch
1 package (3 ounces) strawberry-flavored gelatin
Whipped cream, for serving

Bake the pie shell until golden brown. Set aside to cool. Wash and hull the strawberries and drain well. Slice the strawberries and place in the cooled pie shell. Set aside.

Combine the water, sugar, and cornstarch in a saucepan. Cook over medium heat, stirring constantly, until mixture comes to a boil. Continue to cook over low heat until mixture is thick and clear, about 2 minutes. Add gelatin. Stir until the gelatin is dissolved. Pour hot mixture over the strawberries. Chill until set. Best when served hours later. Top with whipped cream.

Note: This recipe can also be made by substituting fresh raspberries and raspberry-flavored gelatin.

Strawberry Shortcake

3 pints fresh strawberries
½ cup plus 2 tablespoons sugar, divided
2¼ cups flour
4 teaspoons baking powder
¼ teaspoon salt
⅓ cup shortening
1 egg
⅔ cup milk
2 cups heavy cream, whipped

Preheat oven to 425 degrees. Grease and flour a round cake pan. (An 8-inch pan will make a thicker cake.) Wash, hull, and slice the strawberries. Toss strawberries with ½ cup sugar. Set aside.

In a medium bowl, combine the flour, baking powder, remaining 2 tablespoons sugar, and salt. Cut in the shortening until the mixture looks like crumbs. Make a well shape in the center of the flour mixture. In another bowl, beat the egg and add the milk. Add the milk mixture to the flour mixture. Stir until just combined. Pour the batter into the pan. Bake until a toothpick inserted in the center comes out clean, 15 to 20 minutes. Let the cake cool on a wire rack.

When the cake has cooled, slice it in half carefully to make two layers. Place half of the strawberries on one layer, and place the other layer of cake on the strawberry layer. Place the remaining strawberries on the top. Cover the strawberries with whipped cream.

Strawberry Sauce for Ice Cream

4 cups fresh strawberries
1 cup sugar
1 teaspoon vanilla

Wash and hull the strawberries. Cut the large berries in half. Put the strawberries, sugar, and vanilla in a medium saucepan over medium heat. Bring to a gentle boil and cook, stirring constantly, until the berries are soft, about 5 minutes. Take the pan off the heat and mash the berries with a potato masher. Add a little water if the sauce seems too thick. Return the mashed sauce to low heat and cook for 2 minutes or until done as desired. Skim some of the foam off the sauce with a spoon if desired before serving. Store in the refrigerator.

CHAPTER 18

FROM THE VINES

Along with Ma's strawberries, we picked wild berries throughout the summer, some for Ma to use in baked goods or preserves, and some to eat—sometimes right there where we stood among the berry bushes. Ma also grew a couple rows of red raspberries in a patch near the barnyard next to the asparagus.

Wild grapes grew in our woodlot on long, heavy vines that tangled around the oaks and climbed thirty feet or more to the top of some of the trees. In a good season with plentiful rain, we had lots of wild grapes.

Ma liked wild grapes for making jelly, but beyond jelly she didn't know what to do with them. One summer, when the wild grapes hung heavy and after the grape jelly jars were filled, Ma decided to bottle up some of the grapes with warm water. She had no recipe, but I'm sure she had grape wine on her mind. On a back shelf in the cellar stood a dozen or so empty brown bottles—I believe now they were left over from Prohibition days. Ma and Pa chucked the plump little grapes into the bottles, covered them with warm water, and then capped the bottles with a bottle capper we happened to have (also left over from Prohibition?). They then carried the filled bottles to the basement, lined them up on a basement shelf, and pretty much forgot about them.

A few weeks later, all of us were awakened to the sound of an explosion. Pa quickly determined the location of the loud noise was the cellar. Upon observing the shelf with the bottles of grapes lined up in a row, he quickly saw that one of them had blown up, scattering glass all about. He gently carried one of the intact bottles upstairs, and as we all gathered in the kitchen, he asked Ma to hold it while he opened it with the pliers he always carried with him. With the cap removed, partially fermented grapes shot out of the bottle like machine gun bullets, just missing Ma's nose before they struck the ceiling and then began raining down, along with the odorous juice. It happened so quickly that Pa just stood there with an astounded look on his face, and Ma with an empty bottle in her hands, wondering what was dripping down on her head.

My brothers and I began laughing, for it was about the funniest thing we'd seen since the last Fourth of July when we blew up the neighbor's mailbox with a firecracker. Pa had a grin on his face too. But not Ma. All she could see was a fermented grape mess all over the kitchen ceiling, table, and floor.

Pa retreated to the cellar and, using the outside cellar door, carried the remaining bottles outdoors, where we opened them and allowed the grapes to shoot out on the lawn. Ma's experiment had failed. But fermented grapes raining down from the kitchen ceiling remains one of our best family stories.

No wild blueberries grew on our farm, nor did we see them on any of the neighboring farms. But about twenty-five miles west, in Adams County, we found ample amounts. Pa had been born and spent his early years on a farm in Adams County, so he remembered picking wild blueberries and knew exactly where to find them.

On a warm August day, Ma packed a lunch, and we gathered up milk pails, piled into the Plymouth, and were off for a day of blueberry picking. Unlike the cultivated variety, wild blueberries are tiny, about the size of a pencil eraser, so it took a lot of picking just to cover the bottom of a milk pail with berries. The main problem for my brothers and me was putting the blueberries in the pails rather than in our mouths. The juicy little purple berries were so sweet and tasty that we even managed to ignore the hot sun baking our backs and the relentless mosquitoes drilling into our hides as we enjoyed the berry feast. We did manage to return home with a few pails of wild blueberries, most of which Ma canned. But she also made a wild blueberry cobbler that was just the best.

Blackcaps (or wild raspberries) grew along the edge of our woodlot and along our fencerows, in the tangle of brush, small trees, and stone piles. If the spring rains had been ample, the supply of blackcaps could be several pails full, more than the birds could steal. Usually in July, after the strawberries quit bearing, the blackcaps turned from little red nubbins to jet black berries

MAKING GRAPE WINE

A few years after the exploding-bottles-of-grapes experience, we had another bumper crop of wild grapes. This time, my aunt Louise offered a recipe for making balloon wine, which my mother made several times. I can't say it was my favorite wine, but she and Pa had a good time making it and offering it to friends and relatives who stopped by on occasion. And on the positive side, none of the wine bottles blew up.

HOMEMADE BALLOON WINE

6–8 pounds of grapes
1 package (5 grams) red wine yeast (Eleanor might have used crumbles of cake yeast)
2 cups sugar
Empty bottles with lids
Colander
Cheesecloth
One-gallon jug
Large, sturdy balloon

1. Wash grapes and remove stems.
2. Place grapes in a bowl and mash them to break the skins.
3. Place mashed grapes in a cooking pot and heat with low heat for about 30 minutes.
4. Remove from the heat. Add 2 cups of sugar to the warm grape juice and stir until sugar is dissolved.
5. Strain the grape juice through a colander lined with cheesecloth.
6. Pour the juice into a clean gallon jug and allow to cool at room temperature.
7. Add red wine yeast to the juice.
8. Fasten the balloon over the opening of the jug, tying it firmly in place.
9. Set the jug in a warm, dry area. The juice will begin to ferment in a couple of days, and as it ferments the balloon will expand.
10. In about 40 to 60 days, the balloon will deflate completely. When it does, siphon the wine from the jug into clean bottles. Cap the bottles. Store in a dry, dark area until ready to serve.

the size of the tip of a little finger. They are a native fruit, like blueberries and cranberries, that grow wild in Wisconsin and many of the northern states. Blackcaps are more firm than blackberries, which also grow in the wild. Pa preferred blackcaps over blackberries, as the blackcaps were sweeter and had much smaller seeds. They were also easier to pick than shade-loving blackberries, which we found only deep in the woods.

If it had rained overnight and it was too wet to continue making hay, Ma would ask if we'd like to pick some blackcaps. Having worked in the fields since early spring, we knew where the blackcaps grew; we'd kept an eye on them, watching them ripen. Ma must have been doing a little reconnoitering on her own, as she also knew when the blackcaps were ripe. Although her way of introducing the topic made it sound like we had a choice in the matter, we knew she wanted it done. She had three little empty Karo syrup pails and lengths of binding twine already prepared. We ran the binder twine through the pail's handle and then tied it around our waists. "Allows you to pick with both hands," Ma reminded us. "No sense having to hold the pail with one hand and pick with the other."

So Donald and Darrel and I would trudge off to the patch of blackcaps along the fencerow leading to the night pasture. Ma had warned us that there should be none of the "one for the pail, and one for the mouth" kind of picking. But it was impossible to avoid checking on the ripeness of the fruit we were picking without occasionally eating one.

Picking blackcaps had its virtues—well, one virtue: you could stand up while picking them. But there were many negatives. The plant's briars tore at your skin. Walking among stone piles was not only difficult, but you never knew what you might discover (we were most concerned about snakes, even though the snakes we encountered were usually as afraid of us as we were of them). It took forever to fill the little pail we had tied to our waists, because the berries were so small. What kept us going, besides the fact that we had no choice, were thoughts of Ma's blackcap pies and the blackcap sauce that we would bring up from the cellar in the dead of winter, reminders of those blistering hot and humid days when we stumbled among the stone piles and wire fences to capture the sweet black berries.

Compared with picking wild blackcaps and blackberries, picking red raspberries was easy. They ripened about the same time as the wild varieties, and when they did they were a deep red and oh so good to eat. You could stand up to pick them, and you could mostly avoid the inevitable scratches that came with picking wild berries.

Not to be confused with blackcaps, blackberries may look similar but are quite different. Both berries are red when immature and dark black when ripe. But after picking, blackcaps are hollow, and blackberries are solid. Blackberries are two or three times larger than blackcaps, with considerably larger seeds. Pa never cared for blackberries, mostly because their large seeds found their way under his dentures.

Blackberries grew deep in our woods, on brambles that grew six feet tall and taller and were covered with thorns designed to keep away all but the most zealous pickers. They also grew in patches, usually in an open place in the woods where there was more sunlight. A blackberry patch might be ten yards square, sometimes much larger. One look at a blackberry patch and any sane person would declare it impenetrable. Yet that is where Ma sent us when she wanted blackberries. She especially sent us in the direction of the blackberry patches if the blackcaps had not yielded well. We could usually count on the blackberries, which seemed less dependent on ample spring rains than the blackcaps did.

When picking blackberries, we wore long-sleeved shirts, no matter how warm the day, and we still came home with scratches in places where we'd never had them before. Our buckets filled up faster because the berries were larger than blackcaps, but it was difficult to pick with two hands, as one hand was usually busy swatting the mosquitoes that seemed to thrive in the lush blackberry patches.

Wild Grape Jelly

3½ pounds wild grapes (to make about 5 cups of juice)
1½–2 cups water, divided
1 box (1.75 ounces) fruit pectin
½ teaspoon butter
7 cups sugar

Have all jars, lids, rings, and all canning equipment thoroughly clean and in good condition. This recipe makes about seven 8-ounce jars.

Wash grapes and remove the stems. Crush the grapes in a large kettle. Add 1½ cups water. Bring to a boil; reduce the heat and simmer until grapes are soft, about 10 minutes.

Place 3 layers of damp cheesecloth over a large bowl. Transfer the soft grapes to the cheesecloth. Tie the cheesecloth closed. Let the grape juice drip into the bowl until dripping stops or overnight. Measure the juice. If necessary, add up to ½ cup of water to make 5 cups of grape juice. Measure the 5 cups of juice and pour into a 6- or 8-quart pot or canner. Add fruit pectin and butter. Bring to a full rolling boil over high heat, stirring constantly. Quickly add the sugar to the juice and pectin. Bring back to a full rolling boil and let it boil for 1 minute, stirring constantly. Remove from heat and skim off foam with a metal spoon. Pour into sterilized jars, leaving ⅛-inch headspace. Wipe off the jar rims with a paper towel. Cover the jars quickly with flat lids. Screw on the ring bands tightly. Return the jars to a hot water bath in the canner. Be sure the jars are completely covered with water. Let jars boil in water with canner lid on and process for 10 minutes.

Carefully remove jars from the canner and place on a heat-safe towel or other surface. Listen for the "ping" to sound as the lid pops. Check all of the seals. Jars that do not seal properly should be placed in the refrigerator. Store in a cool, dark place. Refrigerate after opening. If you open a sealed jar and it has a bad odor or appears moldy or mushy, discard contents without eating.

Carefully follow all safety and nutrition canning directions included with your jars and consult other canning resources if necessary. When using a pressure canner, follow all directions given by the manufacturer. Food products must be held at high temperature, 10 pounds pressure, to kill bacteria and prevent spoilage. For good basic instructions on canning and preserving, see *Ball Complete Book of Home Preserving*, edited by Judi Kingry and Lauren Devine (Toronto: Robert Rose, 2006).

Raspberry Sauce

    1 pint fresh raspberries, rinsed and drained
    ¼ cup sugar
    2 tablespoons orange juice
    2 tablespoons cornstarch
    1 cup cold water

In a saucepan, combine the raspberries, sugar, and orange juice. In a bowl or measuring cup, whisk cornstarch and water together until smooth. Add the cornstarch mixture to the raspberries. Bring to a boil. Reduce the heat and simmer on low until desired consistency, about 5 minutes, stirring constantly. Remove from heat. The sauce should thicken up as it cools. If desired, carefully pour the hot raspberry sauce into a cheesecloth-covered bowl to remove some of the seeds. Store in the refrigerator.

Blackberry Pie

Prepared pie crust for 2-crust pie

3 cups fresh blackberries, rinsed and drained (If fruit is dry, add
1–2 tablespoons of juice or water. If fruit is bland, sprinkle with
lemon juice.)

¾–1 cup sugar (depending on how sweet berries taste)

2 tablespoons quick-cooking tapioca

1½ tablespoons cornstarch

¼ teaspoon salt

1 tablespoon butter, cut into pieces

A little milk

Preheat oven to 450 degrees. Place one crust in a 9-inch pie plate.

Mix the berries, sugar, tapioca, cornstarch, and salt in a large bowl. Add fruit mixture to the bottom crust in the pie plate. Dot with butter. Add top crust with openings for steam to escape, or arrange lattice strips across the top. Brush the top crust with milk.

Bake for 10 minutes. Then reduce the heat to 350 degrees and bake until crust is golden brown, 20 to 30 minutes longer.

Wild Blueberry Cobbler

BERRIES

2½ cups fresh blueberries, rinsed and drained

½ of a lemon, juiced

1 teaspoon vanilla

1 cup sugar

½ teaspoon flour

1 tablespoon butter, melted

COBBLER

1¾ cups flour

5 tablespoons sugar

4 teaspoons baking powder

5 tablespoons butter

1 cup milk

TOPPING

2 teaspoons sugar

½ teaspoon ground cinnamon

Preheat oven to 375 degrees and lightly grease an 8- or 9-inch-square baking pan.

In a bowl, gently stir the blueberries with the lemon juice and vanilla. Stir in sugar and flour. Mix gently. Pour the blueberries into the baking pan. Sprinkle the blueberries with melted butter. Set aside.

To assemble the cobbler, stir together the flour, sugar, and baking powder in a medium bowl. Cut in the butter using a fork until the dough is in small pieces. Make a well in the center and quickly pour in the milk. Mix until just moistened. Spoon the batter over the blueberries.

To make the topping, mix together the sugar and cinnamon and sprinkle over the blueberries and batter. Bake cobbler until the top is golden brown, about 20 minutes. Let cool a bit before serving.

Perfect Blueberry Muffins

3 cups flour
1 cup sugar
4 teaspoons baking powder
1 teaspoon salt
1 cup milk
½ cup vegetable oil
2 eggs, beaten
1½–2 cups fresh blueberries, rinsed and drained

Preheat oven to 400 degrees and grease a 12-cup muffin pan or line with paper liners. In a large bowl, combine the flour, sugar, baking powder, and salt. In another bowl, mix the milk, oil, and eggs. Add the milk mixture to the dry ingredients. Do not overmix. Batter should be slightly lumpy. Fold the blueberries into the batter. Divide batter among 12 muffin cups. Bake until golden brown, about 20 minutes.

Raspberry Muffins

2 cups flour

⅓ cup sugar

1 tablespoon baking powder

½ teaspoon salt

¾ cup milk plus 2 tablespoons milk

1 egg, beaten

¼ cup butter, melted

½ teaspoon vanilla

1 cup fresh raspberries, rinsed and drained

TOPPING

5 tablespoons sugar

2 tablespoons flour

½ teaspoon cinnamon

½ teaspoon raspberry extract

2 tablespoons butter

Preheat oven to 400 degrees and grease and flour a 12-cup muffin pan or line with paper liners. In a large bowl, combine 2 cups flour, ⅓ cup sugar, baking powder, and salt. In another bowl, whisk together the milk, egg, melted butter, and vanilla. Stir the milk mixture into the flour mixture. Carefully fold in the raspberries. Divide the batter among the prepared muffin cups.

To make the topping, mix 5 tablespoons sugar, 2 tablespoons flour, cinnamon, and raspberry extract. Use a fork to cut in the butter until the flour is crumbly. Sprinkle the crumb mixture on each muffin. Bake until a toothpick inserted into the center of a muffin comes out clean, about 18 minutes.

Blackcap Muffins

6 tablespoons unsalted butter

⅓ cup whole milk

1 large egg

1 egg yolk

¾ teaspoon vanilla extract

1½ cups all-purpose flour

¾ cup sugar

1½ teaspoons baking powder

¾ teaspoon salt

1½ blackcaps, rinsed and drained

Preheat oven to 365 degrees and grease and flour a 12-cup muffin pan or line with paper liners. Melt butter in a small saucepan over low heat; remove from heat. Whisk in milk, egg, egg yolk, and vanilla until well combined.

In a medium bowl, whisk together flour, sugar, baking powder, and salt. Add milk mixture and stir until just combined. Gently fold in the berries. Divide the batter among 12 muffin cups. Bake until golden and crisp and a toothpick inserted in the center comes out clean, about 18 minutes. Cool for 15 minutes, then run a knife around edges of muffin tops and carefully remove from cups.

CHAPTER 19

CHERRIES

About once a week, Ross Caves, Wild Rose's local trucker, hauled a load of livestock raised by the farmers in our community to the stockyards in Milwaukee. In his red cattle truck, he transported hogs, veal calves, worn-out dairy cows—whatever livestock a farmer wanted to sell. But he did much more.

Once a year he scrubbed out his truck, removing every last vestige of animal waste, straw, and dirt. Then he put up a poster at the Wild Rose Mercantile announcing that he would be making his annual trip to Door County for a day of cherry picking. He included a phone number to call for those who wanted to go along. My mother looked forward to the ride in the back of the cattle truck along with other women from the Wild Rose area interested in a day away, a day for socializing and a few hours of cherry picking. My mother's sisters, Aunt Louise and Aunt Arvilla, went too.

Even though Ross placed folding chairs in the back of his truck, the 130-mile trip to Sturgeon Bay was long, often hot, always bumpy, and, according to my mother, one of the most fun things she did all year. After arriving at one of Door County's orchards, they spent the rest of the day picking cherries, taking time out for a break to eat the bag lunches they had brought along.

My mother returned home with two or three milk pails (sixteen quarts each) filled with ripe red cherries. My dad, my brothers, and I, plus a very tired Ma, spent the next couple of hours pitting the cherries, one at a time, each of us using a hairpin, which Ma said worked best for removing the pits.

The next day Ma canned cherries, baked a cherry pie, and made cherry cobbler. During the long, cold days of winter, Ma often asked one of us to fetch a jar of cherry sauce from the cellar. It was a special dessert treat, for my mother not only tasty but also filled with memories.

PITTING CHERRIES

Use a simple, black metal hairpin, the kind with a U-bend. Remove the stem from the cherry. Push the ends of the hairpin into the cherry, making sure the ends are on either side of the cherry pit. Then push until the ends pop out of the other side of the cherry. Grab the ends and pull them all the way through, bringing the pit along with the hairpin.

Cherry Delight

2 cups pitted sour cherries
1¼ cups water, divided
1 cup plus 2 tablespoons sugar, divided
3 tablespoons cornstarch
40 regular-size marshmallows
1¼ cups milk
1½ cups heavy cream, whipped
1½ cups graham cracker crumbs
⅓ cup butter, melted

Preheat oven to 350 degrees and grease a 9 x 13-inch pan. Combine cherries, 1 cup water, and 1 cup sugar in a saucepan. Heat on medium heat and simmer for 5 minutes. In a bowl or measuring cup, whisk together ¼ cup water and cornstarch. Stir into the cherry mixture. Let cool.

In a double boiler or in a metal mixing bowl set over a saucepan of simmering water, dissolve marshmallows in milk. Let cool. Add whipped cream to the cooled marshmallow mixture.

Mix melted butter and remaining 2 tablespoons sugar with the cracker crumbs. Put crumb mixture in bottom of pan, saving enough for a light layer on top. Pour half of marshmallow mixture over crumbs, then spoon cherry mixture over the entire surface. Add the rest of marshmallow mix and top with the rest of the crumbs. Bake until the top browns, about 40 minutes.

Canned Cherry Sauce

Eleanor canned most of the cherries that she picked in Door County. She used a water bath kettle for canning, following these directions from her recipe card.

> 8–10 pounds of cherries (1 pound equals about 2 ½ cups)
> 2–3¼ cups of sugar

1. Wash the cherries in cold water. Remove the pits.

2. Wash the jars and rings. Only use new lids. Place the canning jars in water bath kettle, boiling them for 10 minutes. Keep the jars in hot water until used. Put the rings and the lids in a pan of hot water until ready to use.

3. After removing the pits, place the cherries in cold water with 2–3 tablespoons of lemon juice to prevent discoloration.

4. Prepare the syrup. Use 3¼ cups of sugar and 5 cups of water. In a large kettle, combine the sugar and water. Bring to a boil over medium-high heat, stirring until sugar is dissolved. Reduce heat to low.

5. Add the pitted cherries to the syrup and bring back to a boil and cook for about 5 minutes, stirring constantly.

6. Put the cherries and syrup into the jars. Fill each jar to within ½ inch of the top. If there is not enough liquid to cover the berries, add additional boiling water. Slip a knife in the inside edge of each jar to let out air bubbles.

7. Wipe the top edge of the jars so the lids will seal. Place a new lid on the jar and gently tighten the ring.

8. Place the jars in the canning water bath, so they are completely covered with water.

9. Bring the water to a boil and process in the boiling water canner. Boil pint jars for 15 minutes and quart jars for 20 minutes.

10. After the processing is completed, carefully lift the jars out of the water and let them cool overnight. Once the jars are cool, check the lids to be sure they have sealed. They should be flat. If the jar is not sealed, keep in the refrigerator and enjoy within a week.

Carefully follow all safety and nutrition canning directions included with your jars and consult other canning resources if necessary. When using a pressure canner, follow all directions given by the manufacturer. Food products must be held at high temperature, 10 pounds pressure, to kill bacteria and prevent spoilage. For good basic instructions on canning and preserving, see *Ball Complete Book of Home Preserving*, edited by Judi Kingry and Lauren Devine (Toronto: Robert Rose, 2006).

Cherry Cake

1½ cups sugar
½ cup shortening
½ cup milk
½ teaspoon vanilla
3 egg whites, beaten
3 cups flour
3 teaspoons baking powder
⅓ cup pitted and chopped fresh cherries
¼ cup cherry juice

Preheat oven to 350 degrees and grease a 9 x 13-inch pan. Cream the sugar and shortening in a bowl. Add milk and vanilla and mix until smooth. Gently fold in the beaten egg whites and continue mixing it all together.

Mix flour and baking powder in a small bowl. Gradually add the flour mixture to the batter. Continue folding the flour mixture in a little at a time until all the flour is mixed in. Be careful not to stir. Fold in the cherries and juice. Pour batter into pan and bake until a toothpick inserted in the cake comes out clean, about 40 minutes.

Aunt Louise Witt, picking apples

CHAPTER 20

THE HOME ORCHARD

Most of our neighbors had a few apple trees. Some of the folks who had moved to our neck of the woods from Rose, New York, back in the 1850s brought with them apple trees that they planted here. Tom Stewart, who in 1867 homesteaded the farm I own now, and who came from Rose, is believed to have brought New York trees with him that he planted in a small orchard in back of his cabin. One of those trees remains, although it is battered and torn and no longer bears apples.

My pa started a small orchard when he and my mother moved onto the home place in 1924. He planted it on a little hill almost directly across the road from the farmhouse, making it easily accessible. We grew several varieties: Russet, Northwestern Greening, Wealthy, and Whitney Crab. I don't recall Pa spraying the trees; if we found a worm in an apple, we simply cut or ate around it. I do remember Pa saying, "Biting into an apple and finding a worm is far better than finding half a worm."

Starting in late August and into September, we picked apples—not a lot of them, but enough for eating and for our school lunch pails, and enough for Ma to make such treats as apple pie, apple crisp, and many jars of applesauce.

Pa was proud of our little orchard. Two or three larger commercial orchards were nearby, but we never visited them or bought apples from them. It was one more case of our growing what we needed and not having to depend on others to grow things for us.

Apple Crumble

4 cups cored, peeled, and sliced apples
½ cup packed brown sugar
½ cup quick-cooking oats, uncooked
⅓ cup flour
¾ teaspoon cinnamon
¼ cup butter
Ice cream or whipped cream, for serving

Preheat oven to 350 degrees and grease an 8 x 11-inch pan. Arrange apple slices in the pan. Set aside.

Combine remaining ingredients. Stir until crumbly and sprinkle over the apples. Bake until lightly browned, 30 to 35 minutes. Serve with ice cream or whipped cream.

Apple Kuchen

1¼ cups flour
2 teaspoons sugar
1 teaspoon baking powder
1 teaspoon salt
½ cup plus 3 tablespoons butter, divided
1 egg
2 tablespoons milk
4–6 baking apples, peeled, cored, and cut into eighths

TOPPING
¾ cup sugar
½ cup flour
½ teaspoon cinnamon

Preheat oven to 350 degrees and grease a 9 x 13-inch baking pan. In a large bowl, mix 1¼ cups flour, 2 teaspoons sugar, baking powder, and salt. Cut ½ cup butter into the dry mixture, blending until crumbly.

In a small bowl, beat the egg with milk. Add this to the dry mix. Mix thoroughly. Pat the dough into the baking pan. Place the apple slices on the dough in rows until all of the dough is covered. Dot the apples with the remaining 3 tablespoons of butter.

To make the topping, mix sugar, flour, and cinnamon together. Sprinkle the topping over the apples. Bake until golden brown, 30 to 45 minutes.

Ma's Apple Pie

Dough for two 9- or 10-inch pie crusts (recipes on page 168)
¾ cup sugar, plus a little for sprinkling on top crust
1½ tablespoons quick-cooking tapioca
1 teaspoon cinnamon
⅛ teaspoon salt
6 cups peeled and sliced apples
2 tablespoons butter
1–2 tablespoons milk
Vanilla ice cream, for serving

Preheat oven to 425 degrees. In a large bowl, mix sugar, tapioca, cinnamon, and salt. Put the sliced apples in the sugar mixture and mix together. Set aside and let sit.

Roll out a pie crust and place it in the bottom of a 9- or 10-inch pie tin. Place the apple and sugar mixture in the pie crust. By this time, the apple in the sugar mixture will be a little juicy. Dot the apples with butter, slicing little bits around top of the apples.

Roll out second layer of pie crust. Cut slits in the top pie crust or cut out pieces with a cookie cutter, such as a holiday or an apple shape. Place on top of filling and crimp around the edges to seal the two crusts together. Brush the top crust with milk using a pastry brush. Sprinkle the top crust with white sugar.

Bake the pie until filling bubbles with heavy bubbles that don't break, 50 to 55 minutes. You might want to bake the pie on a cookie sheet in case it bubbles over. The filling will sometimes bubble up through the slits. If this happens, the pie is done! Serve with vanilla ice cream.

Family Apple Pan Pie

8 cups peeled and sliced apples
1 tablespoon lemon juice
1 cup plus 2 tablespoons sugar, divided
3 tablespoons quick-cooking tapioca
2 teaspoons cinnamon
Prepared crust for a 2-crust pie (see recipes on next page)

Preheat oven to 350 degrees. In a large bowl, mix the apples and lemon juice.

In a separate bowl, combine 1 cup of the sugar, tapioca, and cinnamon. Add the sugar mixture to the apples. Stir together and set aside.

Roll out two-thirds of the pie crust and place in the bottom and sides of a 10 x 16-inch jelly roll pan. Spread apple filling evenly on the crust. Roll out the remaining pie crust and place on top of the apples (it will be thin). Seal the edges. Sprinkle the top with remaining 2 tablespoons of sugar. Poke holes in top crust with a fork.

Bake until pastry is golden brown, about 60 to 70 minutes. Cool slightly before serving.

Pie Crust with Oil

1¾ cups flour
1 teaspoon salt
½ cup oil, plus a little extra if needed
3–4 tablespoons cold water or milk

Put flour and salt into a bowl. Add oil and mix. Add water or milk 1 tablespoon at a time. Do not add more water if dough seems dry; add a few drops of oil instead. Divide dough in half for two 8- or 9-inch crusts. Roll out between pieces of wax paper.

Quantity Pie Crust

4 cups flour
1 tablespoon sugar
1½ teaspoons salt
1½ cups lard (or other shortening)
1 egg, beaten
1 tablespoon vinegar
½ cup water

Mix the flour, sugar, and salt together in a large bowl. Cut in the lard until dough is the size of peas. Add the vinegar and the water to the egg. Sprinkle the egg mixture over the flour mixture, 1 tablespoon at a time. Toss it with a fork to mix it in. Gather the dough with your fingers so it pulls away from the sides of the bowl. Leave the dough in the bowl. Chill before rolling. This recipe makes enough for three 9-inch pie crusts.

Applesauce

About 8 medium cooking apples (to make about 4 cups of pulp)
1 cup sugar
¾ teaspoon cinnamon

Put some water in a large kettle, enough to cover the bottom of the pot. Cut up apples and remove the cores and seeds. You don't need to peel the apples. Fill the pot ¾ full with apples. Bring the water to a boil over medium heat. Then reduce heat and simmer the apples until they are soft, 5 to 10 minutes.

When the apples are soft, put them through an applesauce colander— a cone-shaped aluminum sieve that has a wooden pestle masher to push the soft apples through. The skins will remain in the colander and the soft apple will go through. Remove any remaining skins from the kettle. Put the sieved soft apples back into the kettle. Add the sugar and cinnamon.

Bring the apple mixture to a boil, stirring constantly. Reduce heat and let the apples simmer for 4 to 5 minutes. Stir often to prevent the applesauce from sticking to the bottom of the pot. Store in the refrigerator.

To can the applesauce, put it into clean, hot, sterilized jars, leaving 1-inch headspace. Seal with sterilized new lids and clean, hot rings. Put the jars in a boiling water bath for 25 minutes. Cool jars away from drafts. Store in a cool, dark cupboard.

Carefully follow all safety and nutrition canning directions included with your jars and consult other canning resources if necessary. When using a pressure canner, follow all directions given by the manufacturer. Food products must be held at high temperature, 10 pounds pressure, to kill bacteria and prevent spoilage. For good basic instructions on canning and preserving, see *Ball Complete Book of Home Preserving*, edited by Judi Kingry and Lauren Devine (Toronto: Robert Rose, 2006).

CHAPTER 21

CANNING MEAT, VEGETABLES, AND FRUITS

We had no electricity on the home farm when I was growing up, and thus no freezer in which to preserve food, so Ma had to can everything she wanted to preserve, including vegetables, fruits, and meats. She managed to do all of her canning on the wood-burning cook stove, using a boiling water canner that held several quart jars.

Depending on when various vegetables and fruits were ready, Ma canned several times during the summer, sometimes twice a week. My brothers, Donald and Darrel, were usually called upon to help Ma with the canning, as I was doing field work with Pa. Canning days were usually Wednesday and Thursday. (Monday and Tuesday were saved for washing clothes and ironing, and Friday was for straightening up and cleaning the house for the possibility of city visitors' coming unannounced on the weekend.)

After working the morning in the fields, when Pa and I returned to the house for the noon meal, we were treated to a very hot kitchen and the wonderful smells associated with whatever might be going into the canning jars. The preparation for and the canning process were slightly different for each fruit or vegetable.

Most of what Ma canned came from our garden, our orchard, or from the wild berry patches we visited, but Ma did buy at least one crate of pears and a box of peaches for canning. Every summer Ma bought pears and peaches from the Wild Rose Mercantile. She preferred Colorado peaches and would wait for Arnol Roberts at the Mercantile to call when the Colorado peaches came in. Thankfully the two fruits did not arrive at the same time. Ma would spend a whole day canning pears and another entire day canning peaches when they were at their ripest. These fruits came in wooden boxes that had to be pried open—Pa's job—before the fruit, each pear or peach wrapped in tissue paper, could be removed.

Of the many things that Ma canned, I especially enjoyed the strawberry jam and the peaches and pears. As I got older, dill pickles also became one of my favorites. Thanks to Ma's hard work over the hot stove, we all enjoyed her canned vegetables and fruits, jams, and jellies throughout our long Wisconsin winters.

CANNING BASICS

Canning is a method of preserving food by processing it in boiling water for a set amount of time and sealing it in airtight jars. This sterilizes the bacteria that cause spoilage and allows you to store the food longer. To avoid food poisoning, especially botulism caused by the bacterium *Clostridium botulinum*, low-acid foods such as vegetables, meats, and poultry either should be processed in a pressure canner to make certain bacteria are killed during processing or should be pickled, a process that increases the acid content (see page 181). My mother did not use a pressure canner—they hadn't come along yet—but she did add acidic ingredients such as vinegar and lemon juice to low-acid foods when canning with the boiling water bath method. High-acid foods, such as berries and other fruits, can be safely preserved in a boiling water canner.

Canning procedures vary some from food to food, but here are some general instructions for canning. Be sure to follow the manufacturer's directions included with your canning equipment. For more detailed instructions on canning and preserving, see *Ball Complete Book of Home Preserving*, edited by Judi Kingry and Lauren Devine (Toronto: Robert Rose, 2006).

Always use jars, lids, and screw bands that are specifically made for canning, such as Kerr and Ball jars. These jars have a special neck design to fit the screw bands. (Do not recycle and use other glass jars, such as vintage canning jars or mayonnaise or spaghetti sauce jars and lids.) The top of the jar must be smooth, with no cracks, chips, or breakage. The jars need to fit completely inside your canning pot. Canning lids are made to lie flat and seal the top of the canning jar; do not reuse lids for canning. The screw band should fit tightly and hold the lid in place securely.

BOILING WATER METHOD

High-acid foods are processed by a method of canning that uses boiling water, which heats the jar and its contents to a temperature of 212 degrees. These foods can be processed using the boiling water method:
- Soft spreads: jelly, jam, and fruit butters
- Tomatoes: tomato juice, tomato sauce, crushed tomatoes (no vegetables or meat added to the tomatoes)
- Fruits: in syrup, fruit juice, or water

- Pickles: The acidity level is raised by fermentation or by adding vinegar. The higher acidity level helps to preserve the food.

A boiling water canner is a large, deep pot with a lid. Inside is a rack to hold the jars, suspending them and allowing them to be surrounded by boiling water. The rack has handles that hook onto the pot. The pot has to be large enough so that the water covers the jars by three inches.

To prepare for boiling water canning:
- Check your jars and screw bands for breakage or misshape.
- Wash the jars and screw bands in soapy water and rinse clean.
- Place the jars in the rack of the pot. Fill the pot with water. Bring the water to a boil. Boil for 10 minutes. Turn off heat. Leave jars in hot water until ready to use.
- Place the new, flat lids and screw bands in a separate pot with water. Bring the water to a boil. Turn off the heat and let the lids and bands sit in hot water until ready to use. Remove the jars and lids carefully with a tongs to avoid burning your hands.

ADDITIONAL CANNING TIPS
- Wear an apron and keep your hands and the kitchen area clean.
- Use a wooden cutting board area as a "filling station." Don't set a hot jar on a cold surface when filling it with hot food.
- A wide-mouth funnel can be handy for filling jars.
- Use paper towels to wipe clean the rim and threads of each jar after filling to ensure a tight seal.
- Use a kitchen knife to slip in the side of each jar to release air bubbles before putting on the lid and screw band.
- Use a thick dishcloth to turn the hot screw bands tightly after filling. Turn the band until it is just finger tight. Do not overtighten or use a tool to tighten the band.
- Prepare an area for the hot canned jars to rest, such as on a dishcloth, to protect the surface underneath from heat.

Canned Crushed Tomatoes

Fresh-picked tomatoes
Lemon juice
Salt

Prepare canner, jars, lids, and screw bands for the boiling water method of canning (see page 172).

Fill a pot with water and bring to a boil. Put a small number of tomatoes in the boiling water to blanch them for 60 seconds until the skins start to crack. Carefully remove the tomatoes with a slotted spoon. Quickly put them in a bowl of cold water in the sink. Slip the skins off and discard the skins. Cut out the cores and remove any bruised or brown spots. Continue blanching other tomatoes you are planning to can.

Working in batches, slice enough tomatoes to measure 2 cups. Put the sliced tomatoes in a pot and bring to a soft boil over medium heat. Smash the tomatoes with a potato masher while they are cooking. Continue adding sliced tomatoes 2 cups at a time until all are being cooked. Stir to be sure they are not sticking to the bottom of the pot. When all tomatoes are in the pot, boil for 5 minutes.

Add 1–2 tablespoons of lemon juice to each quart jar just before filling with the hot tomatoes. (Add less juice for a pint jar.) Put hot tomatoes in the hot, prepared jars. Press the tomatoes in, leaving no large spaces or air pockets. Leave ½-inch headspace. Wipe the rim. Center the lid on the jar with one hand and tighten the screw band with your other hand. Place the jars in the canner, being sure they are completely covered with hot water. Bring the water back to a boil and process quart jars for 45 minutes or pint jars for 35 minutes. Carefully remove the jars and put on a heat-safe surface. Let cool. Store in a cool, dry place.

For good basic instructions on canning and preserving, see *Ball Complete Book of Home Preserving*, edited by Judi Kingry and Lauren Devine (Toronto: Robert Rose, 2006).

Strawberry Jam

    2 quarts ripe strawberries, at room temperature
    7 cups sugar
    1 package (1.75 ounces) of fruit pectin (not the liquid kind)
    1 teaspoon butter

Prepare canner, jars, lids, and screw bands for boiling water method of canning (see page 172). This recipe makes enough for eight 8-ounce jars.

Put sugar in a bowl and set aside to have ready to add to cooking berries. Wash and hull the strawberries and discard the stems. Put berries in 9 x 13-inch cake pans in a single layer. Crush them with a potato masher. Measure crushed berries and juice to make 5 cups berries. Put crushed berries in an 8-quart kettle and stir fruit pectin into the fruit. Add butter to reduce foaming. Bring fruit mixture to a full rolling boil, stirring constantly, with a long wooden spoon, until it keeps on boiling when you stir it. Carefully add the sugar. Return the berries to a full rolling boil, stirring constantly. Boil for 1 minute. Remove from heat. Skim any foam off the top with a metal spoon.

Immediately fill a prepared jar with jam, leaving ¼-inch headspace. Wipe off the jar rim and threads. Cover the jar with the lid and a screw band. Hold the lid down with one finger and screw the lid tight with a towel. Turn the jar upside down on a cloth on the counter. Continue filling other jars. When all jars are filled, turn them right side up. Listen for a "ping" when the lids pop. This means the tops are sealed and the jars are ready for storage.

For good basic instructions on canning and preserving, see *Ball Complete Book of Home Preserving*, edited by Judi Kingry and Lauren Devine (Toronto: Robert Rose, 2006).

Raspberry or Blackberry Jam

2 quarts fresh raspberries or blackberries (to make 5 cups of
crushed berries)
7 cups sugar

Prepare your canner, jars, lids, and screw bands for boiling water method
of canning (see page 172). This recipe makes about nine 8-ounce jars.

Crush the berries. Sieve half of the pulp through a cone-shaped canning
strainer sieve to remove some of the seeds, if desired. Follow the canning
instructions for Strawberry Jam (page 175) in a hot water bath (boiling
water method).

Blueberry Jam

3 pints blueberries (to make 4 cups crushed berries)
4 cups blueberries
4 cups sugar
2 tablespoons lemon juice

Prepare your canner, jars, lids, and screw bands for boiling water method
of canning (see page 172). This recipe makes about six 8-ounce jars.

Remove stems and crush the berries. Follow the canning instructions
for Strawberry Jam (page 175) in a hot water bath (boiling water method).

Canned Pears in Syrup

About 10 pounds ripe (but not too soft) pears
5¼ cups water
2¼ cups sugar

Prepare your canner, jars, lids, and screw bands for boiling water method of canning (page 172). This recipe makes four 1-quart jars or eight 1-pint jars.

In a pot, combine the water and sugar. Bring to a boil over medium heat, stirring constantly until the sugar is dissolved. Turn the heat to low and keep the syrup warm.

Peel, core, and cut the pears in half. In a large pot, layer the pears in syrup. Warm them about 5 minutes until they are heated all the way through. Use a slotted spoon to remove the pears.

Pack a jar with the hot pears in layers. Use a spoon to fill the jar with hot syrup. Each quart jar will have 1 to 1½ cups of syrup. Leave ½-inch headspace. Remove air bubbles with a kitchen knife. Center the lid on the jar with one hand and tighten the screw band with the other hand. Place the jar in the canner. When all jars are full and in the canner, be sure they are completely covered with water. Bring to a boil. Process pint jars for 20 minutes and quart jars for 25 minutes with the cover on. Remove the cover and let rest for 5 more minutes. Carefully move jars to a heat-safe surface to cool. Store in a cool, dark place.

For good basic instructions on canning and preserving, see *Ball Complete Book of Home Preserving*, edited by Judi Kingry and Lauren Devine (Toronto: Robert Rose, 2006).

Canned Peaches

About 10 pounds ripe Colorado peaches
5 cups water
3¼ cups sugar

Prepare your canner, jars, lids, and screw bands for boiling water method of canning (see page 172). This recipe makes four 1-quart jars or eight 1-pint jars.

To peel peaches, place them in a pot of boiling water for about 1 minute, until the skins begin to crack and split. Using a slotted spoon, carefully move the peaches from the hot water to a bowl of cold water. Slip the skins off with your hands and discard. Slice the peaches in half. Remove the pits.

In a pot, combine the water and sugar. Bring to a boil over medium heat, stirring constantly until the sugar is dissolved. Turn the heat to low and keep the syrup warm.

One layer at a time, place the peaches in the pot of syrup over warm heat. Heat about 1 minute until heated through. Using a slotted spoon, layer hot peaches into a hot jar. Spoon hot syrup in the jar to cover the peaches. Leave ½-inch headspace. Remove air bubbles with a thin, nonmetal spatula. Wipe the rim and threads of the jar with a paper towel. Center the lid on the jar with one hand and tighten the screw band with the other hand. Place the jar in the canner. When all jars are full and in the canner, be sure they are completely covered with water. Bring to a boil. Process pint jars for 20 minutes and quart jars for 25 minutes with the canner cover on. Remove the cover and let sit for 5 minutes. Carefully move jars to heat-safe surface to cool. Store in a cool, dark place.

For good basic instructions on canning and preserving, see *Ball Complete Book of Home Preserving*, edited by Judi Kingry and Lauren Devine (Toronto: Robert Rose, 2006).

UNEXPECTED USES FOR PEAR
AND PEACH CRATES

The pears and peaches Ma bought every summer came in wooden crates. After the pears and peaches were canned, Pa saved the crates for other uses. He knew that when Uncle Charlie and Aunt Sophia came for their summer visit, Uncle Charlie would use a pear crate to make a kite for my brothers and me. He used the thin wood to make the kite frame and then covered it with newspaper glued together with paste he made by mixing wheat flour and water. For string, we used the huge ball of string Ma saved from the purchases she had made at the Mercantile, and for the tail we strung together hunks of old shirts and underwear. With hundreds of feet of Ma's string, and with Uncle Charlie's careful instruction, we flew kites so high that they were only a speck in the sky.

Wooden peach crates also hold a special place in my memory. During the six months when I couldn't walk or attend school after suffering a bout of polio, Pa made me a little desk from two peach crates he stood on end with a board nailed across the top. It was at my makeshift desk that I did the schoolwork that my teacher, Mrs. Jenks, brought out to the farm each day so I could keep up with my studies. It wasn't a fancy desk, but at the time it was very special, and it's something I've never forgotten.

CHAPTER 22

CUCUMBERS, PICKLES, AND PICKLING

Cucumbers were a major cash crop for our family, and we grew a half acre to an acre or more of them every year. Pa planted the pickle patch (as we called the cucumber field) close to the farm buildings, so with just a few steps we could be in the patch to hoe. When the cucumbers were ready for picking, we picked every third day or so, depending on the temperature and the amount of rainfall.

You could always spot someone who picked cucumbers, as the vegetables left a greenish crust on your hands that was near impossible to remove, even with the strongest soap. Picking cucumbers was hard work, bending over with the hot sun on your back for four or five hours, searching for the cucumbers that always seemed to hide beneath the scratchy leaves. We picked cucumbers in five-gallon pails; when the pail was full, we dumped it into a burlap bag, and when each bag was full, we tied it with a length of binding twine. At day's end we hauled the filled bags to the house with the tractor and wagon and then, after supper and when chores were done, we loaded the four or five bags into the back of the Plymouth and drove them over to the H. J. Heinz Cucumber Salting Station in Wild Rose. There they were sorted into five grades (number ones were the smallest, fives were the largest). After sorting, the

Dill Pickles
from Elenor

Pour Boiling Water over pickles let stand for 10 min then make a brain of 3 qts water and 1 qt vinegar and 1 cup salt boil and of salt pour put over over pickle pack in jar + Seal.

cucumbers were weighed and dumped into silo-like vats for curing. We received our checks for the cucumbers before we left for home.

We saved plenty of cucumbers for Ma to make into pickles. Ma canned many jars of pickles, mostly dill pickles, but also beet pickles, crabapple pickles, and sweet-and-sour pickles and relishes.

CANNING PICKLES

Pickles are canned using the boiling water method (see page 172 for more instructions). Pickling cucumbers and other low-acid vegetables adds enough acid to preserve them through fermentation or the addition of vinegar. Pickled vegetables still need to be processed in a boiling water canner to destroy bacteria that cause spoilage.

Using the correct amount of sugar, salt, vinegar, and spices is critical to the quality and safety of your pickled vegetables. Be sure to follow directions and use adequate processing times for each type of food you are pickling.

PICKLING BASICS
- Follow all manufacturers' instructions for jars, lids, and screw bands. Wash jars, lids, and screw bands thoroughly in hot, soapy water and rinse. Use new seal lids. Keep the lids and screw bands warm in a pot of warm water so they will be warm when you are ready to place them on the hot jars.
- Place the jars in the rack of the pot. Fill the pot with water. Bring the water to a boil. Boil for 10 minutes. Turn off heat. Leave jars in hot water until ready to use.
- Fill hot jars with pickles/relish, leaving ½-inch headspace. Be sure the added liquid called for in the recipe completely covers the contents of the jar. Wipe off the rim and threads of the jar with a paper towel.
- Press the lid on the jar with one hand and tighten the screw band with your other hand.
- Hold the hot jars with a dish towel or a potholder and place carefully back in the rack. Be sure the water in the canner covers the jars by 2 inches.

(Continued next page)

(Continued from page 181)

- Return the water to a boil; start timing after the water is at a rolling boil. Be sure to process for the entire recommended time.
- Carefully remove jars from the water using tongs. Let jars cool on a heat-protected surface.
- Check all of the seals. Jars that do not seal properly should be placed in the refrigerator.
- Store properly sealed jars in a cool, dry place. Refrigerate after opening.
- If you open a sealed jar and it has a bad odor or appears moldy or mushy, discard the contents without eating.

ADDITIONAL PICKLING TIPS

- Always use fresh vegetables that are free from bruises and soft spots.
- Wash thoroughly and cut out any soft spots.
- Use white distilled vinegar for the best color. Cider vinegar may make the pickles look dark.
- Use fresh spices when possible. Fresh dill rather than dried dill is best for dill pickles.
- Use white sugar, not brown sugar.

Sweet-and-Sour Pickles

3 pounds cucumbers (3–4 large cucumbers)
6–8 cups water, or more if needed to cover cucumbers
½ cup salt
2 cups vinegar
2 cups sugar
1 yellow onion, sliced thin
1 tablespoon mustard seed
1 teaspoon celery seed
1 teaspoon pepper
1 teaspoon turmeric

Prepare your canner, jars, lids, and screw bands for the boiling water method of canning (see page 172). The number of jars you need will depend on the size of the cucumbers. Wash the cucumbers. Check for soft spots and cut off. Slice the cucumbers into ⅛-inch slices.

Combine water and salt in a large bowl. Stir until the salt dissolves. Add the cucumber slices. Be sure they are covered with water. Cover the bowl and refrigerate overnight or up to 24 hours. The next day, drain the cucumbers but don't rinse them.

Place the vinegar and sugar in a large pot and cook over medium heat until the sugar dissolves.

Add the cucumbers, onion, mustard seed, celery seed, pepper, and tur-meric to the pot and bring the mixture to a boil. Turn off the heat and ladle the hot cucumbers into prepared jars. Leave ½-inch headspace. Seal the jars with prepared clean lids and screw bands.

Place the jars in the canner. They must be covered by 2 inches of water. Cover the canner and boil for 10 minutes. Carefully remove the jars and let cool on a heat-safe surface. Store in a cool, dry place. If the lids did not seal, store the jars in the refrigerator. Refrigerate after opening.

For good basic instructions on canning and preserving, see *Ball Complete Book of Home Preserving*, edited by Judi Kingry and Lauren Devine (Toronto: Robert Rose, 2006).

Beet Relish

8 cups chopped or ground cooked beets

4 cups chopped or ground raw cabbage

3 cups sugar

3 cups vinegar

1 cup ground horseradish (use more or less, according to your taste)

3 teaspoons salt

⅛ teaspoon pepper

Prepare your canner, jars, lids, and screw bands for boiling water method of canning (see page 172). This recipe makes about ten 1-pint jars.

Mix all ingredients together in a large kettle. Bring to a boil. Carefully pack boiling mixture in hot sterilized jars. Place jars in the canner and cover with water. Cover the canner and boil for 15 minutes. Remove the jars and let cool on a heat-safe surface. Store in a cool, dry place.

For good basic instructions on canning and preserving, see *Ball Complete Book of Home Preserving*, edited by Judi Kingry and Lauren Devine (Toronto: Robert Rose, 2006).

Refrigerator Pickles

8 cups sliced cucumbers (leave the skin on)
1½ tablespoons pickling salt
2 onions, sliced into rings
2 cups sugar
1 cup white vinegar
1 teaspoon celery seed
1 teaspoon mustard seed

Place cucumbers and pickling salt in a large bowl and mix together. Let stand for 30 minutes. Drain off any resulting liquid and rinse cucumbers with water. Let cucumbers rest in a bowl of fresh water for 1 hour. Drain again. Put cucumbers in a 3-quart container with a cover. Add onions.

In a medium saucepan, combine sugar, vinegar, celery seed, and mustard seed. Heat over medium heat, stirring until the sugar dissolves. Pour the hot mixture over the cucumbers and onions. Let cool. Cover and store in the refrigerator. These pickles will keep for several weeks.

Dill Pickles

30–34 small cucumbers
3 cups cider vinegar
3 cups water
6 tablespoons pickling salt
Fresh dill or dill seed
Garlic cloves or ⅛ teaspoon garlic powder
6 teaspoons mustard seed

Prepare your canner, jars, lids, and screw bands for boiling water method of canning. This recipe will make 3 or 4 quarts of pickles.

Wash the cucumbers and set aside. Combine the vinegar, water, and salt in a large pot. Bring to a boil to make brine.

Place 3 or 4 bunches of dill (or a teaspoon of dill seed), 1 garlic clove (or a pinch of garlic powder), and 1½ teaspoons mustard seed in the bottom of each warm, sterilized quart jar. Pack the cucumbers in jars, filling halfway. Add another 3 or 4 bunches of dill or a teaspoon of dill seed. Fill the jars to the top with cucumbers. Carefully pour boiling vinegar brine into each jar, leaving ½-inch headspace.

Wipe the top of the jar with a paper towel. Place a lid on the jar with one hand and tighten the screw band with the other hand. Place the jar in the canner. Be sure all of the jars are covered with water. Process the jars for about 20 minutes. Remove the jars and allow to cool on a heat-safe surface. Store in a cool, dark place. The pickles may shrivel after processing. They will later plump up in the sealed jar.

For good basic instructions on canning and preserving, see *Ball Complete Book of Home Preserving*, edited by Judi Kingry and Lauren Devine (Toronto: Robert Rose, 2006).

Apple Pickles 1

From Eleanor's recipe card, no directions included!

6 cups water
5 cups sugar
2 cups vinegar
A few whole cloves
Red food coloring

Apple Pickles 2

This recipe from Eleanor's recipe box has a few more instructions. Make this recipe using canning instructions for boiling water method (page 172).

2 gallons cleaned apples
6 cups sugar
1 quart vinegar
2 cups water
2 tablespoons whole cloves

Mix the apples with sugar, vinegar, water and whole cloves. Fill large roaster with apples and pour mixture over the apples. Bake in 350 degree oven for 1½ to 2 hours or until apples start to pop open. Make a light syrup with 2¼ cups sugar and 5¼ cups of water. Cook the water and sugar over medium heat until sugar is dissolved. Reduce the heat and keep warm until needed.

Pack into jars and cover with hot syrup. Seal jars with clean lids and screw bands.

PART THREE

GATHERINGS AND HOLIDAYS

CHAPTER 23

VISITING

Grandpa and Grandma Witt lived about a mile and half from our farm, closer if you walked across the fields to get there. One of my earliest memories is walking along our dusty road alongside my mother, who was pulling my baby twin brothers in a wagon, on our way to Grandma's house. To me it seemed like a long trip, but not an unpleasant one, as there was always a rabbit or a squirrel to see or birdsong to hear. A car might even pass us, though this was unlikely, as our country road saw little travel except for the milkman and the mailman on their daily routes. My mother always seemed to enjoy visiting with her mother, and of course Grandma and Grandpa liked to see how the twins and their big brother were doing.

I liked visiting Grandma's house too because, unlike us, they had electricity. It was generated in their pump house by a gasoline engine that powered a generator, which sent the electrical power to a huge bank of glass batteries that took up one entire end of the building. I learned later that it was a Delco 32 volt system, and it provided enough power so that Grandma and Grandpa had electric lightbulbs and Grandma was able to iron with an electric iron. I suppose I became a nuisance, turning the light switches on and off to see the bulbs light up and go out again. At home kerosene lamps and lanterns provided our light; they were hot and dangerous, nothing like a fancy light switch that could be snapped on and off.

What I remember most about my visits to Grandma's house was her sugar cookies. She always had a fresh batch made, and they were so good. I also remember how much Grandma Witt enjoyed our visits. Country life, for women especially, could be lonely, and visitors were always welcomed in

and offered something to eat. My mother had cookies or cake on hand, for she knew that often a neighbor would come calling, especially on long, dreary midwinter days.

My pa never cared much for several of Ma's relatives, especially her cousin's family who lived in Wisconsin Rapids. The husband had a good-paying job in a paper mill, and they lived several notches better than we did, meaning they had electricity, a furnace to heat their home, and indoor plumbing, all things that we lacked on the farm. But what galled Pa most was their attitude. They knew they were better off than we were, and they made no bones about letting Pa know that. As Pa saw it, we were aware they had more conveniences than we did, but they didn't have to rub it in. Besides, if they really wanted to push the issue of who was better off and who wasn't, Pa wasn't afraid to say, especially to Ma, how sorry he was for that poor bugger who had to spend his days in a smelly, noisy paper mill while Pa got to work outside where the air was clean and fresh, and didn't smell like rotten eggs.

A visit to Grandma Witt's

One time when we visited them in their fancy city house, Ma's cousin offered my brothers and me milk from their refrigerator. The only time we had cold milk to drink was in the wintertime, but here we were with cold milk in front of us, and it wasn't even fall. That cold milk tasted so good that my brothers and I drank every last drop that they had. I overheard Ma's cousin whisper to her, "Don't you let your boys drink milk? I thought you had a dairy farm." Ma was so embarrassed, she didn't know what to say—but she certainly did not want to point out that her cousin's refrigerator kept milk a lot colder than our icebox did.

When we planned a visit to the city cousins, Ma would write ahead, making sure they knew of our plans. But these folks liked to pop in to see us unannounced. I recall one of their visits, on a cool early October Sunday. After our noon meal, Pa and I had planned to go rabbit hunting. We were just about to sit down to eat when Ma's cousin and her family pulled into the yard and parked under the big elm tree near the kitchen door.

"Well, don't that beat all," Pa said. I knew his thoughts contained stronger language, as his face said a lot more than did his words. I saw my chance to go hunting with Pa fading along with the driveway dust that settled after the cousin's husband shut off his Chevrolet.

Ma went to the door and let them in, greeting them like she was well aware that they were coming. She seated the whole bunch in the rarely used parlor—Ma's way of showing her city relatives that we weren't as bad off as they thought.

Pa and my brothers and I were stuck talking to our "shirt tail" relatives, as Pa called them, while Ma hustled to put together a noon meal for four more people. After a short while Ma called us to the table, where she had laid out, with a few minutes' notice, a wonderful noon meal. Good thing we had plenty of canned meat, vegetables, and fruit stored in the cellar.

After we finished eating, we all gathered once more in the parlor. The husband sat in one of Ma's big "visitor" chairs and promptly fell asleep. So there was Pa, trying to remain friendly and patiently waiting for them to leave so he and I could go rabbit hunting. About two or so, the cousin woke up, the whole kit and caboodle crawled into their Chevrolet, and Ma told them how much she appreciated their coming. Pa and I waved and smiled—glad that they had finally decided to leave so we could go hunting.

MENU

Dinner for Unexpected Visitors

Canned chicken heated with butter in the cast-iron skillet	*Canned strawberries served in Ma's "fancy china" bowls*
Canned peas or corn	*Sliced apple cake*
Homemade bread and butter	*Coffee*

Family friends George and Mable Renkert, who lived in Chicago, spent George's two-week vacation with us on the farm every summer. George was a longtime Chicago postman. He and Mable had no children, and even though my brothers and I never heard them say it, we knew they enjoyed being around kids.

When the Renkerts visited, Ma prepared more German food, as both of them were very German, including speaking to my mother in German. Pa, who was half German, understood some of the language but couldn't speak it. So I rather enjoyed the puzzled look on Pa's face when the Renkerts talked to Ma in German and Pa could pick up only the odd word or two. (It was the Renkerts who taught me the few German phrases I know, including *Vogelnest im baum*, which means bird nest in the tree—a phrase that hasn't been all that valuable when I want to show off my German prowess to German speakers.)

We also enjoyed visits with our neighbor Alan Davis, who lived with his daughter, Katherine, about three quarters of a mile north of our farm. He often came visiting on a cold winter day—unannounced, but Pa and Ma always welcomed him, for he usually had a story to tell, and he enjoyed my mother's baking.

I think Ma welcomed Alan's visit as much as he enjoyed stopping by, as winter days could be lonely. He walked, of course. Everyone walked in those days, especially on cold winter days when starting a car often proved a challenge. If he came on Saturday and we weren't off ice fishing, I'd often sit in on the conversation. Alan would usually arrive shortly after the noon meal, hang his Mackinaw coat on a hook near the cookstove, and park himself on a chair right next to the stove.

I remember one particular Saturday afternoon when Alan had settled in, lit up his corncob pipe, and began spinning stories. When Pa and Alan began telling stories, it was clear that competition for the best story was on.

Somehow the discussion got around to how deep the frost had gone into the ground that year. Pa talked about how difficult it was for the gravediggers, who had to build a fire over the grave site and let it burn for most of a day before the ground was thawed enough so the dirt could be turned. Alan then shared what he'd heard about how they handled the problem up north, where the frost went even deeper into the ground. "Those gravediggers didn't go to all that trouble building a fire to draw the frost out of the ground," he said.

With the big smile on his face, as he knew he had walked right into the middle of Alan's story, Pa asked, "So what did they do?"

"One of the taverns had an unheated storage room in the back. When somebody died, they just laid him on a shelf in that room until spring. The body was frozen stiff, so it'd keep until the temperature warmed up. When the ground thawed, the graves were dug and the bodies laid to rest."

We all laughed at the thought of it, wondering what it must have been like to visit that storage room in winter, as those who worked in the tavern had to do from time to time.

Grandma Witt's Sugar Cookies

A note at the top of this recipe card refers to it as a "State Fair winner."

   2 cups sugar, plus a little to sprinkle on top of cookies
   1 cup butter
   1 teaspoon vanilla
   ⅔ teaspoon baking soda
   ½ teaspoon salt
   3 eggs
   3⅔ cups flour, plus a little for rolling out
   2 teaspoons baking powder

Beat the sugar, butter, vanilla, baking soda, and salt in a large bowl until creamy. Add eggs to the creamed mixture. In another bowl, sift together the flour and baking powder. Add gradually to the creamed mixture. Chill dough before rolling out.

Preheat oven to 425 degrees and grease and flour a cookie sheet. Cut out cookies on a floured surface. Put a little sugar on top. Bake until brown, about 8 minutes.

Sliced Apple Cake

2 eggs, beaten
1 cup white sugar
1 cup brown sugar
½ cup shortening
1 cup milk
2 cups flour
1 teaspoon baking powder
1 teaspoon cinnamon
½ teaspoon salt
2 cups sliced baking apples

TOPPING
½ cup sugar
½ cup chopped nuts
½ teaspoon cinnamon

Preheat oven to 325 degrees and grease a 9 x 13-inch pan. In a large bowl, combine beaten eggs with the sugars and shortening and mix well. Add milk and stir. In another bowl, mix flour, baking powder, cinnamon, and salt; add to the sugar and egg mixture. Add sliced apples and mix. Pour the batter into the pan. Mix the topping ingredients and sprinkle on batter. Bake for 1 hour.

Applesauce and Fruit Cake

1 cup sugar

½ cup butter or lard

1 egg, beaten

1 teaspoon vanilla

2 cups flour

2 teaspoons baking soda

½ teaspoon cinnamon

½ teaspoon salt

1½ cups applesauce

1 cup finely chopped dates

1 cup nut meats

1 cup raisins

Preheat oven to 350 degrees and grease a 9 x 13-inch pan. Beat sugar and butter in a large bowl until creamy. Add the beaten egg and vanilla and mix well. In another bowl, mix flour, baking soda, cinnamon, and salt. Gradually mix with the wet ingredients. Mix in the applesauce. Then stir in the dates, nut meats, and raisins. Pour batter into pan. Bake until a toothpick put in the center of the cake comes out clean, about 1 hour.

Gingerbread Icebox Cookies

1 cup butter
1 cup sugar
2 eggs, beaten
½ cup molasses
4½ cups flour, plus more for rolling out
2 teaspoons baking powder
2 teaspoons ground ginger
1 teaspoon cinnamon
½ teaspoon baking soda
½ teaspoon salt
1 teaspoon lemon extract

Beat butter and sugar in a large bowl until creamy. Add beaten eggs and molasses. In another bowl, sift together flour, baking powder, ginger, cinnamon, baking soda, and salt. Add to wet ingredients. Mix together well. Add lemon extract. On a floured surface, form the dough into long rolls. Place in the refrigerator to chill.

Preheat oven to 375 degrees. Slice dough into cookies and bake on a cookie sheet until no indent remains when cookie is touched, 8 to 10 minutes.

German Chocolate Brownies

1 stick butter
2 squares (2 ounces) German baking chocolate
1 cup sugar
2 eggs
½ cup chopped nuts
1 teaspoon vanilla
¾ cup flour
½ teaspoon baking powder
½ teaspoon salt

Preheat oven to 350 degrees and grease an 8-inch-square baking pan. Melt butter and chocolate in a saucepan over very low heat, stirring constantly. Remove the chocolate from the heat, put in a bowl, and add the sugar. Add one egg and mix well with a fork. Then add the other egg and mix until all of the egg is incorporated. Add nuts and vanilla. In another bowl, sift together the flour, baking powder, and salt. Add the flour mixture to the chocolate mixture and mix thoroughly.

Pour into the pan. Bake until brownies begin to pull away from the edge of the pan, 25 to 30 minutes. Remove from the oven and cool on a rack. Cut into squares while still warm. Remove from pan when completely cool.

Butterscotch Oatmeal Cookies

1 cup shortening
¾ cup white sugar
¾ cup brown sugar
1 tablespoon hot water
2 eggs, beaten
1 teaspoon vanilla
1½ cups flour
1 teaspoon baking soda
Nut meats
1 package (11 ounces) butterscotch chips
2 cups uncooked old-fashioned oats

Preheat oven to 350 degrees. In a large bowl, cream the shortening, sugars, and hot water. Mix in the beaten eggs and vanilla. In another bowl, mix the flour and baking soda. Gradually add the flour mixture to the sugar mixture. Mix well. Stir in the nuts, butterscotch chips, and oats. Drop dough by spoonfuls on a cookie sheet. Bake until light brown, 8 to 10 minutes.

SHIVAREE

Arlin Handrich farmed a half mile east of us. He lived with his mother, and everyone in the community had decided that he would forever be a bachelor. Then he surprised us. On the last weekend of May 1947, he headed for Milwaukee without telling any of the neighbors why. And he returned with his bride, Lorraine, whom he had married on May 28. Just when we'd all given up on him, there he was, grinning from ear to ear with his new wife on his arm.

Arlin and Lorraine hadn't been back to the Handrich farm but a day or two when I overhead Pa and Bill Miller, our neighbor to the south, talking about the need for a shivaree. I'd never attended a shivaree before, so I was looking forward to it. Word soon spread that on Tuesday evening we should all gather at the Handrich farm around nine o'clock or so, when we thought they had gone to bed. Just about every neighbor turned out, men and women, boys and girls, about twenty in all. We parked the cars some distance down the road and all quietly walked toward the Handrich house. When we saw the light in the upstairs bedroom go out, we knew it was time. Pa and Bill Miller were in charge, so we all waited for the signal. We each carried something that made noise: shotguns, sticks pounding on pots and pans, a deer rifle or two, a few firecrackers left over from the previous year's Fourth of July celebration.

When Pa gave the signal—"Now!"—the quiet evening exploded with noise. Shotguns and rifles shooting into the air. The ringing noise of banging pots and pans. And loud yelling, "Shivaree! Shivaree!"

The upstairs light came on once more, then the downstairs light. Arlin and Lorraine appeared at the door, smiling from ear to ear. Arlin had known a shivaree was coming, he just didn't know when. I'm sure Lorraine wondered what kind of neighborhood she had moved into. She soon found out it was her country neighbors' way of celebrating a new marriage and welcoming her to the neighborhood.

The expectation was that the newly married couple would provide beer for the adults and soft drinks for the children. The visitors brought sandwiches, cookies, and cakes to add to the celebration. It was a wonderful time, albeit a bit noisy at first.

CHAPTER 24

QUILTING BEES AND THE LADIES AID

I knew it was Ma's turn to host the quilting bee at our house when she hauled out the quilting frame from the back closet and, with Pa's help, put the frame together across the dining room table, which had been extended to its full length. For several weeks before this, Ma had been sewing together blocks, which would form the top cover for the quilt. Each quilt would also require a middle layer, called batting, and a bottom layer, one large piece of cloth.

Quilting bees were held one afternoon a week for several weeks in the dead of winter. (As I recall, the quilting bee moved around the neighborhood, each winter at a different home, as they helped each other make new quilts.) A half dozen or more neighbor women walked to our place and helped sew Ma's quilt together. It was a slow, painstaking work. But the women enjoyed it immensely, for a quilting bee was as much a social event as work that needed to be done. Before the women left for home late in the afternoon, Ma prepared a simple lunch for them.

MENU

QUILTING BEE

Chicken salad sandwiches on homemade white bread

Dill pickles

Cookies

Pineapple refrigerator dessert

Coffee

When Ma began cleaning the parlor, I knew one of two things was about to happen: either city relatives were planning a visit, or it was Ma's turn to host the Ladies Aid, an organization associated with Saint Paul's Lutheran Church in Wild Rose. The group numbered about eight or ten, plus the pastor, who always attended.

Pa often joked that to be hired as a pastor in our church, the fellow had to be able to balance a Bible on one knee and a lunch plate on the other. I never observed this pastoral balancing act, as Ma would not let my brothers or me near the Ladies Aid gathering. I considered it some sort of secret society, and it was only years later that I learned what they did at their meetings: a little Bible study, some discussion of how foreign missions needed help, and news about what was going on in the church (depending on how much the pastor was willing to share of his sometimes rather juicy insider information, such as who had not been seen in church recently and why, or possible reasons that the young couple recently married had to move up the wedding date).

After the more formal gathering, Ma served lunch. She wanted her Ladies Aid lunch to be perfect—and if possible just a notch better than the lunch served at the last gathering at another member's home. She even caught on to the idea that if you called the lunch a luncheon it somehow increased its value.

MENU

Ladies Aid Luncheon

Shell macaroni hotdish

Open-faced ham and cheese sandwiches

Whipped lime cottage cheese salad

Dill pickles and refrigerator pickles

Chocolate chip date cake

Coffee

Chicken Salad Sandwiches

2 cooked chicken breasts, chopped

1 cup chopped celery

⅔ cup mayonnaise

½ cup toasted slivered almonds

2 tablespoons diced fresh onion

Dash of vinegar

Sour cream to taste

Salt and pepper to taste

Fresh fruit can be added for flavor: blueberries, sliced grapes, raspberries

Sliced bread and lettuce, for serving

Mix all ingredients together well. Serve on bread with lettuce.

Pecan Finger Rolls

1 cup butter, softened

2 cups flour

¾–1 cup ground pecans

½ cup powdered sugar, plus more for rolling out

2 teaspoons vanilla

Preheat oven to 400 degrees. Beat butter until creamy. Mix in flour, ground pecans, ½ cup powdered sugar, and vanilla. Mix well and set in refrigerator to chill. Roll about a teaspoon at a time in palm of hand to make a finger shape. Bake on cookie sheet until set but not brown, 10 to 12 minutes. When baked, roll in powdered sugar.

Bachelor Button Cookies

2 cups brown sugar
1 cup butter
3 eggs
1 teaspoon vanilla
4 cups flour
2 teaspoons baking powder
1 teaspoon baking soda
1 teaspoon salt

Preheat oven to 350 degrees and grease a cookie sheet. In medium bowl, beat the brown sugar and butter until creamy. Beat in the eggs and vanilla. In another bowl, sift together the flour, baking powder, baking soda, and salt. Stir the sifted ingredients into the butter mixture until well blended. Roll the dough into ¾-inch balls. Place cookies 2 inches apart on cookie sheet. Bake until lightly browned around the edges, 8 to 10 minutes. Allow cookies to cool on the baking sheet for a few minutes before moving to a wire rack to cool completely.

Pineapple Refrigerator Dessert

16 graham crackers, crushed
¼ cup butter, melted
3 tablespoons sugar
32 marshmallows
½ cup sweetened condensed milk
1 cup crushed pineapple, drained
1 cup whipped cream

Grease a 9 x 13-inch pan. Mix crushed graham crackers, butter, and sugar and press into bottom of pan, reserving some of the mixture for the top.

Melt the marshmallows with the milk in a double boiler or in a metal mixing bowl set over a saucepan of simmering water. Cool. Add the pineapple and whipped cream. Spread fruit mixture over the graham cracker mixture. Sprinkle with the rest of the cracker mixture. Set in the refrigerator overnight.

Shell Macaroni Hotdish

2¼ cups shell macaroni
1 pound ground beef
2 tablespoons finely chopped onion
2 tablespoons melted shortening
⅔ cup tomato puree
1 cup canned tomatoes mixed with 1 cup water
1 can corn (16 ounces)
1 can (16 ounces) kidney beans, drained
2 teaspoons salt
Dash of pepper

Preheat oven to 400 degrees. Boil noodles in salty water until tender and drain. Brown the ground beef and onion in melted shortening in a frying pan. Add the tomato puree and the tomato-water mixture. Add corn and kidney beans, if desired. Add the salt and pepper. Add the cooked noodles to coat with the sauce. Stir well. Put the mixture in a baking dish and bake for 1 hour.

Whipped Lime Cottage Cheese Salad

1 can (8 ounces) crushed pineapple
1 package (3 ounces) lime-flavored gelatin
12 marshmallows, cut up fine
2 cups cottage cheese

Drain juice from pineapple and add enough water to juice to make 1 cup liquid. Heat liquid to boiling and dissolve gelatin in it. Add marshmallows to hot gelatin liquid. Let cool.

After gelatin has cooled and partly set, whip into a feather-like consistency. Fold in drained crushed pineapple and cottage cheese. Pour into 2-quart mold and refrigerate until set.

Chocolate Chip Date Cake

1½ cups boiling water
1 teaspoon baking soda
1 cup chopped dates
1 cup sugar
½ cup shortening
2 eggs, beaten
1½ cups flour
¾ teaspoon baking powder
¼ teaspoon salt

TOPPING
1 cup chocolate chips
½ cup chopped nuts
¼ cup sugar

Preheat oven to 350 degrees and grease a 9 x 13-inch pan. Mix the boiling water and baking soda. Pour the water over the dates and let cool.

Beat the sugar and shortening together in a large bowl until creamy. Add the beaten eggs and mix. In another bowl, mix the flour, dates, baking powder, and salt together. Add the flour mixture to the sugar and egg mixture. Pour the batter into pan.

To make the topping, mix the chocolate chips, nuts, and sugar together. Sprinkle over the batter. Bake until a toothpick inserted in the middle comes out clean, about 30 minutes. Cool completely. No frosting needed!

CHAPTER 25

HARVEST TIME

Around the middle of June, Pa would walk out to the hayfield every day, looking at the hay crop and deciding when would be the right time to begin cutting. The crop (alfalfa, red clover, and timothy) had to be at just the right maturity. The weather had to cooperate as well, and Pa spent every evening watching the sunset and keeping track of the wind direction and the cloud formations to decide if we would have a stretch of three or four days of dry weather. Cutting the hay was part of the process, of course, but making sure it would dry just right was the most important consideration. Hay that was put up too green or too damp would mold in the barn's haymow and could cause spontaneous combustion, which meant the hay could catch fire and destroy the barn.

While Pa was waiting for the right time, he tinkered with the old McCormick-Deering five-foot sickle bar mower, adjusting it so everything was well oiled, greased, and in good repair. He sharpened the sickle bar, and he made sure that all of the sickle bar guards, which protected the sickle from striking stones, were straight and true.

While doing the morning milking one clear, sunny June day, Pa announced it was the time to start the haying season. After the morning chores were done, the cows let out to pasture, and breakfast finished, Pa hitched Frank and Charlie, our team of Percheron draft horses, to the mower and headed out to the twenty-acre hayfield across the road from the farmstead. All morning long he drove around and around the field, cutting five-foot swaths of hay, which was thick and tall in the hollows, sometimes a bit scraggly on the hilltops. By that evening, the entire hayfield was cut.

After the evening milking, Pa and I walked out to the hayfield and were engulfed in that wonderful smell of curing hay. We inspected the hay piled deep in the hollows, where it was drying more slowly. We looked at the hay on the hillsides, where the hay already seemed dry enough for raking.

"Hay'll be ready for raking tomorrow," Pa said as we walked back toward the house with the sun slipping toward the horizon. "Looks like tomorrow'll be another sunny day."

And it was. With the morning chores finished, Pa hitched the team to the hay rake, a high-wheeled, rather easy-pulling machine that gathered the mowed hay into long ropelike piles. After Pa had made a round or two, my brothers and I used our three-tined pitchforks to gather the raked hay into bunches, called haycocks, for further drying. The haycocks, about four feet tall when finished, had to be constructed so the wind wouldn't blow them over and the rounded top would shed rain. With one look, Pa could determine if a haycock was made properly, and he'd let us know in no uncertain terms if one didn't meet his standards. There were only properly made haycocks in our hayfield.

We brought with us to the hayfield a water jug, stoppered with a corncob. We kept it under a haycock so it would be out of the sun and remain somewhat cool, but as we built more and more haycocks, we sometimes lost track of the water jug. After a little searching, we always found it.

After Pa finished raking and took the team back to the barn, he joined us in bunching hay into haycocks, a tedious, will-it-ever-end kind of job. Finally, at the end of the day, the four of us stood at the edge of the field and looked out at dozens of haycocks. Pa would say, "Isn't that just something to see?" It was about as close as he ever came to saying something was beautiful.

The next day Pa hitched the team to the steel-wheeled hay wagon, which had a wide wooden rack and high bolsters on each end so that it could haul a considerable amount of loose hay. One person rode on the wagon, driving the team from haycock to haycock and "making the load," while the other three of us pitched haycocks onto the wagon. Like everything in farming, it took some skill to toss a haycock onto the hay wagon, especially when the load was well above our heads. The person making the load had to know what he was doing as well, or the load would tip over on its way to the hay barn.

The day was warm, sweat flowed readily, and hay leaves fell down our necks as we pitched hay onto the wagon. Yet it wasn't a bad job, as it had

Making hay

variety. When we had finished loading the wagon, we crawled onto the hay and rode to the farmstead, smelling the sweet fragrance of fresh hay beneath us, listening to the squeaking of the horse harnesses and the crunching of the steel wagon wheels on the gravel of our country road.

Arriving at the farmstead, we jumped off the wagon and ran to the pump for a long drink of well water. Even better, sometimes we were treated to homemade root beer that Pa and Ma had made and stored in the cellar under the house. Absolutely nothing tasted better than a cool bottle of root beer after a hot day of haymaking.

With our root beers finished, we drove the team to the barn, unloaded the hay into the haymows, and returned to the field for another load. We repeated the process until our twenty acres of hay was cut, raked, bunched, hauled, and stored. By the end of haying season, which usually took us well into mid-July, the barn was filled with hay nearly to the roof—enough, we hoped, to feed our cattle and horses through a long winter.

It was usually only a week or two after we finished making hay that the oat crop was ready for harvesting. Between haymaking and the oat harvest, we hoed potatoes, fixed fence, and helped Ma with the garden. While waiting for the right time to cut the oat crop, Pa made necessary repairs to the grain binder, one of the largest horse-drawn machines on the farm. Similar to the hay mower, the grain binder, also a McCormick-Deering, cut the grain with a sickle. But once the grain was cut—the standing grain was pushed into the sickle bar with a rotating wooden reel—it landed on a slatted canvas conveyor that moved the grain stalks to the part of the machine that made bundles and then, with an ingenious device called a knotter, wrapped a length of binder twine around the bundle, tied it into a knot, and kicked it out onto a bundle carrier.

Every farmer in our community grew twenty to thirty acres of oats. The harvested oat kernels became feed for cows, horses, and chickens, and the oat straw provided bedding for the horses and cows during the long winter months. We also piled oat straw around the walls of our farmhouse (this was called banking the house) to keep out the winter chill. Additionally, the oat crop was a nurse crop for the alfalfa and clover so that the oatfield would become a hayfield the following year.

Just as he did with the hay crop, Pa kept an eye on how well the oats were ripening as harvest approached. The oats ripened more quickly on the hilltops than in the hollows, so it was a tricky decision to determine exactly the right time to cut the crop. Sometimes it was the end of July; more often the crop was ready in early August. We knew that hoeing and helping

A HOMEMADE TREAT

My parents had all the supplies needed to make root beer: a five-gallon crock, a supply of glass beer bottles, and a bottle capper and caps. Most of these items were left over from Prohibition days, when many Wisconsin families made their own beer.

ROOT BEER
16 cups cold water
2½ cups sugar
2 tablespoons root beer extract

Mix the water, sugar, and root beer extract in a food-safe container. Put in a cold place, like the cellar, until cool. Drink and enjoy!

Ma with the garden would stop when Pa hitched Frank and Charlie to the grain binder and headed for the twenty-acre oatfield. After Pa had made a few rounds of the field, the task for my brothers and me was to stand up the oat bundles into oat shocks—usually five pairs of bundles stood with their butt ends on the ground.

As in building a haycock, shocking grain took a certain amount of skill so the shocks would stand up against a rainstorm or a strong wind. Pa taught us to take an oat bundle under each arm (they were easy to pick up with the binding twine that held them together), then bend one knee and stand an oat bundle on each side of it, using our hands to push them into place. Then we'd do the same with four more pairs of bundles, alternately placing a pair of bundles on each side of the pair we began with.

Like so many other jobs on the farm, once I got the knack of it, it became just another repetitive and rather boring job for a kid who had other things he'd rather be doing, like going fishing. Once in the morning and once in the afternoon, we stopped shocking grain for lemonade that Ma brought out in the field in a big glass container, along with some of her homemade cookies. We sat under the hot harvest sun, enjoying lemonade kept deliciously cool with ice that Ma had chipped from the icebox. After fifteen minutes or so of rest, it was back to shocking grain, until every last bundle was in a shock. Depending on the growing season, grain shocks now stood everywhere in the field, even on the hilltops if we'd had sufficient rain in April, May, and June. If rainfall had been scant, there would be fewer grain shocks, most of them in the valleys where the soil was heavier.

Lemonade

8 to 10 lemons
6 cups cold water
1 cup sugar
Lemon slices for garnish

Wash the lemons, rinse, and dry. Roll them until soft. Cut each lemon in half and squeeze out the juice. (You will have about 2 cups juice.) Mix the water, lemon juice, and sugar in a large pitcher until sugar is dissolved. Chill if desired. Put a slice of lemon in each glass.

**OPTIONAL METHOD FOR MAKING LEMONADE
WITH A BASIC SUGAR SYRUP:**
In a medium saucepan, combine 1 cup water with 1 cup sugar. This will help dissolve the sugar. Boil for 5 minutes, without stirring. Remove from heat and let cool. Store in the refrigerator in a covered container until you are ready to make lemonade. Add the sugar syrup to the lemon juice and the rest of the water and stir to make lemonade.

Sour Cream Cookies

1 cup butter
1½ cups sugar
2 eggs
1 cup sour cream
½ teaspoon vanilla
4½ cups sifted flour
1 teaspoon salt
1 teaspoon baking soda
1 teaspoon baking powder
½ teaspoon nutmeg

Preheat oven to 375 degrees. Beat the butter in a large bowl until creamy. Add the sugar and beat until light and fluffy.

Add the eggs one at a time and beat well. Add the sour cream and vanilla and mix. In another bowl, sift together the dry ingredients. Add gradually to the sugar mixture and stir. Form the dough into walnut-sized balls and put on a cookie sheet. Bake until lightly browned, 10 to 12 minutes.

Chocolate Chip Squares

1 cup shortening
½ cup white sugar
1½ cups brown sugar, divided
2 eggs, separated
1 tablespoon cold water
1 teaspoon vanilla
2 cups flour
1 teaspoon baking soda
½ teaspoon salt
1 package (12 ounces) chocolate chips
1 cup chopped nuts

Preheat oven to 350 degrees. Grease and flour a 9 x 13-inch pan. Beat the shortening in a large bowl until creamy. Add the white sugar and ¾ cup of the brown sugar. Add egg yolks, water, and vanilla. Beat well. In another bowl, sift together the flour, baking soda, and salt. Add the dry ingredients gradually to the sugar mixture. Mix until it forms a doughlike pie crust. Press the dough into the bottom of the pan. Sprinkle the dough with chocolate chips.

Whip the 2 egg whites until stiff. Fold in the remaining ¾ cup brown sugar, 1 tablespoon at a time, beating quickly until stiff peaks form and sugar is dissolved to form a meringue. Pour this egg and sugar mixture over the layer of chocolate chips. Sprinkle the nuts over the meringue. Bake for 30 minutes. Let cool and cut into squares.

CHAPTER 26

THRESHING DAY

The first thing Pa bought when World War II ended was a new Farmall H tractor. He paid $1,750 for it. The second thing was a used Case thresher that he and our nearest neighbor, Bill Miller, bought together for $282.50. The seller wanted $300, but in those days you never paid full price for something, especially if it was used. I suspect one of the reasons Pa and Bill refused to pay the asking price was because it didn't include a drive belt. Pa bought a new drive belt from Sears and Roebuck for $49.

Everyone in our neighborhood grew oats in those days, twenty or thirty acres, enough to provide straw to bed the cattle during the winter when they stayed in the barn, and to add grain to the corn to make cattle feed (grist, we called it, when the corn and the oats were ground together at the water-powered mill in Wild Rose).

I had been a part of the threshing season since I was a little shaver; one of my first jobs was shoveling oats in our granary's oat bin after men working at the machine carried sacks full of the newly threshed grain to the granary. But now I was old enough to go from farm to farm with Pa and Bill Miller and their threshing machine, threshing oats for the neighbors. Threshing season was akin to a neighborhood celebration, as everyone who had grain to thresh helped everyone else and the threshing machine went from farm to farm, creating enormous straw stacks and filling granary bins with oats.

Threshing season was hard work: forking grain bundles onto a wagon, driving the team and wagon from the oatfield to the threshing machine, tossing the grain bundles into the noisy machine, one after the other—not

overlapping them but not leaving a gap between them—all with the hot sun beating down and sweat streaming down your face and back, and everyone watching to see if you could do it, for after all, you were still a kid. And you discovered that you could do it, even though your arms and back ached and you needed a big drink of water after a load of bundles had been pitched into the maw of the ever-hungry threshing machine.

When noon finally arrived on threshing day, you gave the team a drink from the neighbor's stock tank and tied them to a tree in the shade. Then you splashed some water on your face, cleaned the grime from your hands and arms, and filed into the neighbor's dining room with the rest of the threshing crew, ten or a dozen men and maybe a couple of kids as young as you were. You were treated to one of the finest meals you would ever experience, right up there with Christmas or Thanksgiving. When the meal was finished, everyone went outside, shared a story or two, or just laid out flat on the ground for a half-hour nap before going back to work. On most farms, threshing continued throughout the afternoon, so you would eat an evening meal together as well.

Threshing day in the 1950s

MENU

THRESHING DINNER

Mashed potatoes and gravy	*Date nut bread*
Roast beef or pork roast	*Dill pickles*
Cooked peas and glazed carrots	*Apple pie and cherry pie*
Homemade bread with butter	*Egg coffee*

Aunt Louise and Aunt Arvilla, my mother's sisters, came to the farm the day before we were planning to thresh. The women made pies, at least two different kinds. They baked many loaves of bread and several cakes. They put navy beans in water so they would soften and be ready for cooking the following day. They put the leaves in the dining room table, extending it nearly all the way across the room, with enough places for twelve or fourteen men. They then covered the table with a long tablecloth and began setting the plates, cups, saucers, knives, forks, spoons, and glasses in place.

On threshing day, Aunt Louise returned by seven o'clock to help Ma make the final preparations for the two big meals that would be served to the threshing crew. The roast beef or pork went in the oven by eight (nothing spoiled a good threshing day dinner quicker than tough, undercooked meat). The baked beans soon followed.

Around eleven o'clock, Pa poked his head in the kitchen and informed Ma when the crew would shut down for dinner—usually close to noon, sometimes a few minutes after, as the crew waited for the last load of bundles in the morning to be fed into the threshing machine. Ma started a big pot of egg coffee. Around 11:45 Aunt Louise began cutting the meat. Ma was busy mashing potatoes and making gravy. Then Aunt Louise sliced homemade bread and put a plate of it at each end of the long table, along with two smaller plates of butter. The dill pickles went on the table; the pies were cut and set aside, ready for serving when the main course of the meal was finished. As the men filed through the kitchen and into the dining room, Ma would put the gravy and sliced meat on the table.

Quickly the men and boys found their places to eat. When they were all seated, they began passing the dishes around the table and digging in. When a bowl or platter was empty, Ma took it to the kitchen for refilling. There was little talking, as the men were hungry after the hard work of the morning. Coffee was poured and cups refilled. Then it was time to serve the pie—each pie was cut into five pieces, so each piece was ample. (Men complained when the pieces of pie or cake were too small—they wouldn't say so at the table, but the message usually found its way back to the cook.)

When the workers had eaten their fill, they thanked Ma and Aunt Louise and filed back outside. Only then did the women have a chance to eat, before tackling the huge piles of dirty dishes to be washed. In an hour or so,

A MIDWEST TRADITION

For large work crews and big family gatherings, Ma always made boiled egg coffee in a big blue enamel coffee pot that sat on the back of the wood-burning cookstove. Egg coffee was made popular in the Midwest by immigrants from Scandinavia, but most women in our community knew how to do it, no matter their ethnic background. Ma learned how to make it from her mother.

EGG COFFEE
2 cups of coffee grounds
1 egg, beaten
1 cup extra-cold water, divided

Fill the coffee pot about two-thirds full with cold water and place on the woodstove. Mix coffee grounds with beaten egg in a small bowl. Stir until the egg and grounds are moist. Add up to ½ cup cold water if you need to, to be sure the grounds are moist.

When the water in the coffee pot comes to a full boil, add the coffee grounds mixture. Stir constantly to prevent the coffee from boiling over. Boil for 3 to 5 minutes. The longer it is boiled, the stronger the coffee will be. Remove the coffee pot from the heat. Let the coffee pot sit so the grounds settle to bottom of the pot. You can add ½ cup cold water at this point to help the grounds settle faster. Pour the coffee through a fine-meshed sieve or strainer into small coffee pot to serve. Enjoy! The coffee smells great.

they would begin planning for the supper, which was considerably easier than preparing the dinner.

MENU

THRESHING SUPPER

Sliced bologna with homemade bread

Baked beans

Coleslaw

German chocolate cake with coconut frosting

Sugar cookies

Roast Beef

Choose a 3- to 4-pound rump or chuck roast. (For a threshing dinner, make 2 or 3 roasts.) Preheat oven to 325 degrees. Roll the roast in flour and season with salt and pepper. Brown the roast on all sides in hot fat. Add ½ cup cold water. Place the roast in a roasting pan with the fat side up to keep the meat moist. Cover and cook for 2½ to 3 hours, adding more water if needed so the roast does not dry out. Add small onions and peeled and cut carrots during the last 45 minutes.

Beef Gravy

Scrape the drippings from the roasting pan and add potato water (water used for boiling potatoes) to make 3 cups of liquid. Melt 3 tablespoons butter in a frying pan. Add 3 tablespoons flour and 1½ teaspoons salt. Slowly add the drippings and potato water mixture to the pan. Continue to stir until thick and season with salt and pepper to taste.

Glazed Carrots

About 10 medium carrots
¼ cup hot water
3 tablespoons butter
3 tablespoons brown sugar
Paprika

Preheat oven to 350 degrees. Wash and peel the carrots. Cut into bite-size pieces. Cook in boiling salted water until tender. Drain and put in a 1½-quart casserole dish.

Put ¼ cup hot water in a pot. Add the butter and brown sugar. Cook for 5 minutes. Brush the butter mixture over the cooked carrots and bake for 30 minutes. Baste with the butter mixture halfway through cooking. Sprinkle with paprika.

Date Nut Bread

1 cup chopped pitted dates
1 cup boiling water
1 teaspoon baking soda
½ cup shortening
½ cup sugar
1 egg
½ teaspoon vanilla
1¾ cups flour
½ cup chopped nuts

Preheat oven to 350 degrees. Grease two small loaf pans. Put dates in a small bowl and pour boiling water over them. Add the baking soda and stir. Let cool.

Beat the shortening, sugar, egg, and vanilla in a large bowl until creamy. Add the flour alternately with the cooled dates, mixing well. Add the nuts and mix well. Pour the batter into the pans. Bake until a toothpick inserted in the middle comes out clean, 30 to 40 minutes.

Cherry Pie

Prepared pie crust for 2-crust pie
¾ cup sugar, plus more for sprinkling on top crust
3 tablespoons cornstarch
¼ teaspoon salt
⅔ cup cherry juice
3 cups cherries, washed and pitted
2 tablespoons butter
½ teaspoon lemon juice
⅛ teaspoon almond extract

Preheat oven to 350 degrees. Place one crust in a pie dish. Mix the sugar, cornstarch, and salt together in a bowl. Pour into a saucepan, add the cherry juice, and stir. Cook over low heat until thick and clear. Stir in the cherries, butter, lemon juice, and almond extract and remove from heat. Cool. Put cherry mixture in prepared pie crust.

Top with lattice made from strips of pie dough. Flute the edge. Sprinkle the top with a little sugar. Bake until crust is brown and juice begins to bubble up around the crust, 40 to 50 minutes.

Baked Beans

1 pound dried navy beans
⅓ to ½ pound bacon, cooked and diced (optional)
¼ cup brown sugar
¼ cup ketchup
⅓ cup chopped onions
3 tablespoons dark molasses
1 teaspoon salt
1 teaspoon prepared mustard

Place beans in a large bowl, cover with water, and soak overnight.

Preheat oven to 300 degrees. Rinse and drain beans. Put the beans in a saucepan and add enough water to cover them. Bring to a boil, reduce heat, and simmer 20 to 25 minutes. Put beans and liquid in a 2-quart casserole. Add remaining ingredients, combining well. Cover and bake until beans are tender and flavors are blended, 6 to 7 hours. Remove cover for the last 30 minutes. You can adjust the molasses, ketchup, and sugar amounts for your family's taste.

German Chocolate Cake

½ cup boiling water
4 ounces sweet baking chocolate
2½ cups flour
1 teaspoon baking soda
1 teaspoon salt
2 cups sugar
1 cup butter, softened
1 teaspoon vanilla
4 eggs, separated
1 cup buttermilk
Coconut Frosting (recipe follows)

Preheat oven to 350 degrees and grease two 9-inch-square cake pans. Pour the boiling water over the chocolate in a bowl. Stir the chocolate until it melts. Let cool. In another bowl, mix the flour, baking soda, and salt. Set aside. Separate the yolks from the whites.

In another bowl, beat the sugar, butter, and vanilla until creamy. Mix in the egg yolks one at a time. Mix the chocolate into the sugar mixture and blend well. Mix in the flour mixture alternately with the buttermilk until the batter is smooth. Beat the egg whites and fold into the batter. Pour the batter into pans. Bake until a toothpick inserted in the center comes out clean, 40 to 45 minutes. Cool. Remove the cakes from the pans, spread one layer with half of the Coconut Frosting, place the other layer on top and spread with the rest of the frosting.

Coconut Frosting

1 cup sugar
1 cup evaporated milk
½ cup butter
3 egg yolks
1 teaspoon vanilla
1⅔ cups flaked sweetened coconut
1 cup chopped pecans

Mix the sugar, milk, butter, egg yolks, and vanilla in a saucepan. Cook over low heat, stirring until thick, about 15 minutes. Remove from heat. Stir in the coconut and pecans. Continue mixing until the frosting is blended. Let cool before frosting cake.

CHAPTER 27

SILO FILLING AND CORN SHREDDING

Silo-filling season followed threshing by several weeks, usually occurring by mid-September when the corn plant was still green and the corn kernels had only partially ripened—they were in the milk stage, which meant if you pierced a corn kernel a milky substance shot out.

Nearly every farmer in our community had a silo, where the cut corn was stored, fermented, and turned into silage for winter feed for the cattle. The silos were wooden and cylindrical, and most were eight to ten feet in diameter and no taller than twenty-eight or thirty feet.

Ross Caves, our local cattle trucker, also did custom silo filling, going around to farms with his silo filler, a machine that cut cornstalks into small pieces and blew them up a metal pipe into the silo. He also owned a Farmall H tractor that powered the noisy machine.

Pa walked out to the cornfield every day starting in early September, checking whether the plants were ready. When he determined the best day for silo filling, he called Caves and set it up. Next he called several of the neighbors who had silos and asked them if they would be able to help out on the day he had selected. In turn Pa would help them when they were ready to fill their silos.

Pa hitched our trusty team of workhorses to the corn binder and began cutting the green corn a couple of days before silo-filling day. The corn binder cut one row of corn at a time, tied the stalks into bundles, and then spit them out onto the ground where they remained until silo-filling day.

Ross Caves arrived at the farm the day before we filled silo. It took an hour or so to bolt the silo filler pipes together and extend them from the filler to the little door at the top of the silo. My brother Don, when he was old enough, often helped Ross with the pipes, as he had no fear of heights. Extending the pipes to the top of the silo required holding on to the ladder with one arm while handling the pipes with the other. Don did so easily; I was petrified and preferred remaining on the ground.

Around nine the following morning, four neighbors arrived with their teams and wagons and headed out to the cornfield to pick up the heavy green bundles and haul them to the silo, where they fed them into the filler, one bundle at a time. Caves made sure everything was operating properly, usually watching from his seat on the Farmall.

Before I was old enough to handle the heavy corn bundles, my job was inside the silo, working with what was called "distributor" pipes. The freshly cut corn tumbled into the silo through these pipes, which I moved around inside the silo to make sure it was evenly distributed as the silo slowly filled from bottom to top. The reason for the careful packing was to make sure that no oxygen pockets remained in the silo. The silage fermentation process

Filling the silo, 1950s

is an anaerobic process, meaning it will not work if oxygen is present. In addition, pockets of oxygen among the corn would allow mold to form, making the chopped corn dangerous to feed to cattle.

As I worked inside the silo, the smell of freshly cut corn was a pleasant one, earthy and rich. It wasn't a bad job, until the silo was almost full. Then the job became a bit scary, especially for a kid who wondered if he might be buried under the roof of the silo as the cut corn continued to be blown into it. Pa wanted to fill the silo as full as possible, as it would settle several feet overnight. When the silo had as much cut corn in it as there was room, and I could still find a place to breathe, I pushed several handfuls of cut corn out the silo window, signaling the crew to stop feeding bundles into the machine. If I signaled too soon, Pa would let me know, because he usually crawled up the silo chute to see how full the structure was and check my work.

With Pa satisfied that the silo was filled to capacity and the machine shut down, I crawled down the silo chute (on an enclosed ladder that was far less daunting than the ladder placed out in the open) and walked to the house, where the men had gathered for the noon meal.

MENU

SILO-FILLING DINNER

Pork roast with gravy and dumplings	*Apple pie*
Home-canned peas and corn	*Spice drop cookies*
Coleslaw	*Egg coffee*

The next day, after the silage had settled several feet, Pa and Ross Caves blew a couple more loads of cut corn into the silo to fill it once more to the top. Before I crawled into the silo to return to my job of making sure the corn was well packed and distributed, Ross ran the silo filler empty for several minutes, which blew fresh air into the silo. This was to make sure that no silo gas (nitrogen dioxide, which forms during the fermentation process) was present. Silo gas is yellowish brown, has a bleach-like odor, and is extremely toxic.

Once the silo was filled, we waited well into October for the rest of the corn to ripen and for the first frosts to aid in drying the cobs and making corn shredding easier. That process began when Pa once more hitched the team to the corn binder and cut the remaining corn—usually twenty acres, sometimes more. When the corn was cut and the bundles spewed out on the ground, my brothers and I would help with shocking on a Saturday. We stood the bundles on end, making what looked like a tepee. When we had a dozen or more bundles in place, we tied a length of binder twine around the top of the shock and then moved on to create the next shock.

Shocking corn was not an unpleasant task, as those October days were often clear and cool, and the woodlots showed off their fall colors. The occasional flock of Canada geese winged overhead, on their way from the breeding grounds in Canada to warmer places for the winter, honking loudly as they passed. There were no bugs to annoy us, nor was it near as hot as when we shocked oats back in late July and August. The drying cornstalks, heavy with yellow ears, had a special, musky smell that was not at all unpleasant.

When all of the shocks were in place, the cornfield was picture perfect, with corn shocks lined up in rows from one end of the field to the other. We left the shocks standing for a week or two, waiting for the stalks and ears to dry even further. Then, usually on a Saturday, Pa would arrange for a fellow with a corn husker/shredder machine to come by, and Pa would once again ask several of the neighbors to help with the project. On the appointed day, they brought their teams and wagons and hauled the dried corn bundles from the cornfield to the shredder.

The corn husker/shredder resembled a threshing machine, but it was smaller. Its purpose was to remove the corncobs from the stalk, husk them, and then elevate the husked corn into a wagon. The stalks and husks were shredded, and the material was blown out a long pipe, either into the top floor on one end of our barn or onto a stack outside. Pa fed the shredded cornstalks to our cattle and then used what was not eaten as bedding in the barn.

When the cob wagon was filled, the team of horses pulled it next to the corncrib and the men forked the yellow cobs into the slatted structure, where they would remain until we hauled them to the mill in Wild Rose and ground them for cattle feed. Shredding corn took about a day, with the neighbors' help, and Ma prepared both a noon meal and a supper meal for the hungry crew.

MENU

CORN-SHREDDING DINNER

Beef roast

Baked potatoes and gravy

Carrots with cream sauce

Cooked rutabagas

Dill pickles

Peach pie

Egg coffee

MENU

CORN-SHREDDING SUPPER

Boiled ring bologna

Fried potatoes

Sauerkraut

Mashed rutabagas with butter

Dill pickles

Chocolate cherry cake

Egg coffee

Pork Roast with Gravy and Dumplings

5 pounds pork shoulder
1 clove garlic
1 teaspoon dried sage leaves
1 teaspoon marjoram leaves
1 teaspoon salt
Pork Gravy and Dumplings (recipes follow)

Preheat oven to 325 degrees. Trim excess fat from the meat. Cut the clove of garlic in half. Rub the pork with the garlic. Sprinkle the meat with a mixture of sage, marjoram, and salt. Place the meat in a roasting pan on a rack, fat side up. It is not necessary to cover the meat or add water to the bottom of the pan. Roast the pork until a thermometer inserted reads 170 degrees, about 25 to 30 minutes per pound. Be sure the thermometer is not inserted near a bone or into fat. Take the meat out of the oven and let it rest for 15 minutes. Keep the drippings in the bottom of the pan for gravy.

Pork Gravy

¾ cup drippings from pork roast

½ cup flour

4 cups water, or use potato water if you are boiling potatoes with
the meal

Salt and pepper

Cornstarch, if needed

Skim the fat from the drippings in the bottom of the roasting pan and discard. Measure the drippings and pour into a saucepan. Stir in the flour and cook until the mixture starts to bubble. Continue stirring and add the water gradually until the gravy is the desired thickness. Season with salt and pepper. Continue to stir and simmer the gravy for 5 minutes. If the gravy becomes too thin, you can add a little cornstarch to thicken it.

Dumplings

1½ cups flour

2 teaspoons baking powder

¾ teaspoon salt

⅛ teaspoon dried sage

3 tablespoons shortening

1 egg, slightly beaten

⅔ cup milk

Mix together the flour, baking powder, salt, and sage. Cut in the shortening. In another bowl, combine the egg and milk. Stir the milk into the dry ingredients gradually until moistened. Drop the dough by tablespoonfuls into boiling gravy. Cook uncovered for 10 minutes. Cover the pan and cook until the dumplings are fluffy, about 10 more minutes.

Spice Drop Cookies

- 1½ cups raisins
- 1½ cups hot water
- 1½ cup brown sugar
- 1 cup shortening
- 2 eggs, well beaten
- 3 cups flour
- 2 teaspoons cinnamon
- 1½ teaspoons baking soda
- 1 teaspoon ground cloves
- ½ teaspoon nutmeg
- ½ teaspoon salt

Preheat oven to 350 degrees. Put the raisins in hot water in a large bowl and let them sit until they are tender (about 10 minutes). Do not drain. Add the brown sugar, shortening, and beaten eggs. Mix together. In another bowl, combine flour, cinnamon, baking soda, cloves, nutmeg, and salt. Gradually add the flour mixture to the sugar mixture. Mix well. Drop the dough by tablespoonfuls on a cookie sheet and bake until light brown, 8 to 10 minutes.

Baked Potatoes

Preheat oven to 350 degrees. Choose well-shaped, smooth potatoes that are about the same size. Scrub the potatoes. Cut off any discolored parts or anything that looks blemished. Rub each potato with shortening for softer skin. Prick each potato a few times with a fork to allow steam to escape while the potatoes are baking. Bake for 1 to 1½ hours. Serve potatoes with butter or sour cream and salt and pepper.

Carrots with Cream Sauce

6–10 carrots
½ cup sour cream
½ cup chopped parsley or chives

Wash and peel the carrots. Cut them into thin slices lengthwise. Cook carrots in boiling salted water until they are crisp tender, 5 to 7 minutes. Drain. Slowly stir in the sour cream and parsley or chives.

Peach Pie

Prepared pie crust for 2-crust pie
5 cups peeled and sliced fresh peaches
1 teaspoon lemon juice
1 cup sugar
¼ cup flour
½ teaspoon cinnamon
2 tablespoons butter
Whipped cream or vanilla ice cream, for serving

Preheat oven to 425 degrees. Place one pie crust into a 9-inch pie pan. In a large bowl, mix the sliced peaches with the lemon juice. In another bowl, combine sugar, flour, and cinnamon and stir into the peaches. Transfer the mixture to the crust. Dot the peaches with slices of butter. Cover with the top crust. Cut slits into the top crust. Seal the edges and pinch together all the way around. Bake until the crust is brown and juice begins to bubble up through the slits, about 40 minutes. Serve with whipped cream or vanilla ice cream.

Chocolate Cherry Cake

½ cup shortening
1½ cups sugar
2 eggs, beaten
¼ cup cocoa powder
2 tablespoons hot coffee
2 cups flour
1½ teaspoons baking powder
1 teaspoon salt
½ teaspoon baking soda
1 cup sour milk or buttermilk
½ cup chopped maraschino cherries
1 teaspoon maraschino cherry juice

Preheat oven to 375 degrees and grease a 9 x 13-inch pan. Beat the shortening until creamy. Add sugar gradually and mix until fluffy. Blend in well-beaten eggs. In a small bowl, mix cocoa powder and hot coffee to form a smooth paste. Blend into the creamed mixture immediately. In another bowl, mix together the flour, baking powder, salt, and baking soda. Add to the creamed mixture alternately with the sour milk or buttermilk and mix well. Stir in the cherries and cherry juice. Pour the cake batter into pan and bake until a toothpick inserted into the middle comes out clean, 25 to 30 minutes.

CHAPTER 28

THANKSGIVING

Thanksgiving was a special day, but it also posed a problem, for the celebration fell right in the middle of deer-hunting season. If we hadn't bagged a deer by Thanksgiving, we hinted to Ma that after the big noon meal, we'd like to squeeze in a couple more hours of deer hunting. Generally Ma supported our hunting—after all, part of our regular diet consisted of meat from the wild. But she couldn't understand why, after she had worked so hard to prepare a fine Thanksgiving meal, we felt the necessity of hunting. "Couldn't you take off one day from deer hunting?" she asked.

Pa never liked turkey, so we didn't raise them, and turkey was not on our Thanksgiving dinner menu. He preferred duck, which he said had more flavor and wasn't as dry as turkey. We tried raising ducks for a few years, but some critter—either a fox or a weasel—would sneak into the duck house and kill them. So we bought a duck for Thanksgiving. Besides the duck and some store-bought cranberries, everything else on the table came from the cellar: canned vegetables, rutabagas, sauerkraut, potatoes, and pumpkins for pumpkin pie.

Ma began preparations for Thanksgiving several days before the celebration. She baked the pies, baked bread, and prepared the duck for roasting, which involved washing it and then keeping it in the icebox until early Thanksgiving morning when it was put in the oven. For both Thanksgiving and Christmas Ma brought out her special dishes: dinner plates, serving plates, cups and saucers, and platters, all in a wild rose pattern. She set the extended dining room table with these dishes along with her silver-plated silverware, also used only for special occasions.

For these holiday events, Pa always sat at one end of the dining room table and Ma on the other end—the one closer to the kitchen. Relatives could sit wherever they chose, and my brothers and I got the leftover places at the table.

For many years Ma invited her sisters, Louise and Arvilla, and their families, including several of our younger cousins, for the Thanksgiving meal. It was a grand time with lots of eating and storytelling—and if we'd already bagged our deer, it was a relaxing afternoon.

MENU

Thanksgiving Dinner

Roast duck with orange sauce

Mashed potatoes and gravy

Sauerkraut

Cranberry relish

Crabapple pickles

Sweet-and-sour pickles and dill pickles

Pumpkin and mincemeat pies

Milk

Coffee

Roast Duck

5-pound duck
2 teaspoons salt
2 teaspoons paprika
1 teaspoon black pepper
1 apple or 1 onion
½ cup butter, melted

Preheat oven to 375 degrees. Pick and clean the duck inside and out thoroughly. Dry the skin with towels. Rub salt, paprika, and pepper into the skin of the duck. Place in a roasting pan breast side up. To overcome the wild taste, put an apple or onion in the cavity. Roast the duck, uncovered, allowing 20 to 25 minutes per pound, about 1½ hours. Spoon half of the melted butter over the duck. Continue cooking for 45 to 55 more minutes. Spoon remaining melted butter and juices from the pan over the duck. Roast 15 to 20 minutes longer, or until golden brown. Remove the onion or apple from the duck before serving. This is delicious served with Orange Sauce for Duck (recipe follows).

Orange Sauce for Duck

4 tablespoons butter
4 tablespoons flour
Pinch of ground cayenne pepper
1 cup stock made from cooking the neck and giblets
1 cup orange juice

Melt the butter in a frying pan and stir in the flour and cayenne pepper until blended. Remove from heat. Add the stock and orange juice and return the pan to the stove. Stir until mixture thickens. Cook for 5 more minutes over medium heat. Drizzle sauce over cooked duck.

Cranberry Relish

4 apples (unpeeled), sliced
2 oranges (unpeeled), quartered and seeded
1 pound fresh cranberries
2 cups sugar
Nuts

In a hand-operated food grinder, finely chop the apples, oranges, and cranberries together. Put in a bowl. Add the sugar and nuts. Refrigerate until ready to serve.

Nut Bread

This is exactly as it appears on Eleanor's recipe card. "Sweet milk" probably meant whole milk.

½ cup sugar
1 tablespoon lard
1 egg
1 pound sweet milk
2½ cups flour
3 teaspoons baking powder
1 cup chopped nut meats

Mix in order given and let stand in pan 45 minutes before putting in the oven.

Pumpkin Pie

Prepared pie crust for 1-crust pie
1½ cups mashed cooked pumpkin
1½ cups milk
1 cup sugar
3 eggs
A little ground ginger
1 teaspoon salt

Preheat oven to 425 degrees. Place crust in a pie tin. Blend remaining ingredients together and pour into crust. Bake until a knife inserted 1 inch from the edge of the pan comes out clean, 45 to 55 minutes. The pie may look soft but will set later.

Mincemeat Pie

1 pound ground beef
1 cup water
3 cups peeled and chopped apples
1 cup whole raisins
1 cup vinegar
¼ cup corn syrup or molasses
1 teaspoon cinnamon
½ teaspoon ground cloves
½ teaspoon nutmeg
Prepared pie crust for 2-crust pie
1 egg
1 tablespoon water

Simmer the ground beef and water in a frying pan for about 10 minutes, but do not brown. Put meat and apples through food chopper. Combine meat mixture, raisins, vinegar, corn syrup, cinnamon, cloves, and nutmeg in a large kettle and simmer for 30 minutes.

Preheat oven to 450 degrees. Fit a pie crust into a 9-inch pie pan. Pour the hot filling into the crust. With a brush dipped in water, moisten the edge of the bottom crust. Top the pie with the second crust. Crimp the two crusts together with a fork to seal. Cut slits into the top crust.

In a small bowl, whisk the egg with the water. Brush the egg mixture over the top crust. Bake for 15 minutes and remove the pie from the oven. Cover the crust edges with strips of foil to prevent overbaking. Reduce the oven temperature to 350 degrees and bake for 30 more minutes. Partially cool on a rack before serving.

CHAPTER 29

CHRISTMAS

As a kid, I thought Christmas was the best celebration of the year; no other event came close. On Christmas Eve, we put up and decorated our Christmas tree, purchased a few days earlier in Wild Rose. The tree was in the dining room, as far as possible from the wood-burning stove. My parents put a few presents under the decorated tree, but we couldn't open them until Christmas morning, and then only after we had finished the milking. Ma decorated the tree with ornaments she'd saved from year to year, along with a copious amount of aluminum icicles, which became popular in the 1930s. Some years we popped popcorn and strung it together with needle and thread to hang on the tree. Of course we had no Christmas tree lights, as we had no electricity, and Pa would not allow a candle in the house—except on birthday cakes—as he was deathly afraid of a house fire.

We milked the cows early on Christmas Eve so we could wash up, put on our good clothes, pile into the Plymouth, and attend Christmas Eve services at West Holden (Norwegian) Lutheran Church, about three miles from our farm. Ma would have preferred attending a German Lutheran church, but we couldn't do that until one was built in Wild Rose in 1941.

When we returned home, Ma treated us to a special Christmas Eve dinner that featured oyster stew as its centerpiece. Both my parents remembered eating oyster stew on Christmas Eve when they were children. I didn't especially like the smell of oyster stew—pork chops smelled better to me. But Ma and Pa said oyster stew was a family tradition, and there would be no complaining. As was true with everything Ma put on the table, we ate it whether we thought it tasty or not. In addition, Ma brought out the Christmas cookies she'd been busy making. My favorites were the date pinwheels and the ones with chocolate drops in their centers.

In addition to the smells of oyster stew and Christmas baking, our farmhouse was filled with expectations and hopes. After the meal we boys went off to bed, though we slept little. Would we get the presents we had asked for?

MENU

CHRISTMAS EVE SUPPER

Oyster stew	*Cheese slices*
Oyster crackers	*Christmas cookies*
Homemade bread with butter	*Milk*
Homemade fruitcake	*Coffee*

On Christmas morning, I was up at first call to help with the milking and the barn chores. Once back in the house, I washed up, and finally we opened the presents that we had so patiently waited for. During the years of the Depression and World War II, my brothers and I received two presents each, one an article of clothing and one that we had selected from the Sears Christmas catalog. I often asked for a book as my special present. As my brothers and I opened our presents, Pa and Ma exchanged the gifts they had gotten for each other, usually a new winter shirt for Pa and perhaps a button-down wool sweater for Ma.

MENU

CHRISTMAS BREAKFAST

Potato pancakes	*Ma's Christmas stollen*
Pancakes with butter and sorghum syrup	*Christmas morning loaf*
Fried bacon	*Coffee*

After opening our presents, we sat down for breakfast. It usually featured pancakes but also included big slices of Ma's special Christmas stollen.

As wonderful as the breakfast was, I was thinking about my presents. If I had gotten the book I asked for, I couldn't wait to begin reading it. But our family had rules, even on Christmas. No one left the table until everyone was finished eating.

We often ate Christmas dinner at the home of one of the relatives: Aunt Arvilla or Aunt Louise (Ma's sisters), Uncle Wilbur (Ma's brother), Uncle John (Pa's brother), or Aunt Irene (Pa's sister). I would rather have stayed home with my Christmas presents, but visiting relatives was important to the folks, especially at Christmastime. By four o' clock we were home and soon out in the barn doing the afternoon chores. The cows needed caring for 365 days of the year, Christmas Day included.

Oyster Stew

1 pint fresh oysters
1 quart whole milk
1 tablespoon butter
1 teaspoon salt
¼ teaspoon pepper

In a small pan, cook the oysters over medium heat in the liquid they come in, stirring constantly until their edges curl. Heat milk in larger pan on low heat. Add butter and stir until melted. Add the oysters and liquid to the milk. Add salt and pepper and heat thoroughly.

Homemade Fruitcake

1 cup sugar
½ cup butter
¾ cup milk
1 teaspoon vanilla
2½ cups flour
2 teaspoons baking powder
4 egg whites, beaten to stiff peaks
1 cup chopped walnuts
1 cup glazed pineapple pieces
1 cup glazed cherry pieces
½ cup flaked coconut

Preheat oven to 325 degrees and grease 2 loaf pans well. Beat the sugar and butter together in a large bowl until creamy. Add the milk and vanilla and stir. In another bowl, mix together the flour and baking powder.

Add the flour mixture to the milk mixture gradually and mix together. Fold in the beaten egg whites. Stir in the walnuts, pineapple pieces, cherry pieces, and coconut. Pour into the prepared pans. Bake until a toothpick inserted into the center comes out clean, 50 to 60 minutes. Cool on a rack. Remove from pan. When each fruitcake is completely cool, you can wrap it in a cloth soaked in wine or brandy and then wrap in foil.

Date Pinwheel Cookies

8 ounces chopped dates

½ cup water

⅓ cup white sugar

1 teaspoon vanilla

2 cups brown sugar

1 cup shortening

3 eggs

4 cups flour, plus more for rolling out

½ teaspoon cinnamon

1 teaspoon baking soda

¾ teaspoon salt

Combine the dates, water, and white sugar in a saucepan. Cook over low heat, stirring constantly, until soft. Add vanilla and stir. Set aside and let cool.

In a large bowl, beat the brown sugar and shortening together until creamy. Beat the eggs and add to the sugar mixture. In a separate bowl, mix together the flour, cinnamon, baking soda, and salt. Add to the sugar mixture and mix until dough pulls away from the sides of the bowl. Divide the dough in half. Roll out one half on a lightly floured pastry cloth to ¼-inch thickness and into a rectangle shape that is about 18 x 12 inches. Spread date mixture on rolled-out dough.

Roll out the other half the same as before. Cover the first dough rectangle with the second. Using your hands, roll up the dough, beginning on the long side, like a jelly roll. Refrigerate or place in a cold place overnight.

Preheat oven to 350 degrees and lightly grease a cookie sheet. Cut the dough into ½-inch slices and put on cookie sheet. Bake for 12 minutes.

Chocolate Star Cookies

½ cup shortening
½ cup peanut butter
½ cup white sugar, plus more for rolling out
½ cup brown sugar
1 egg
2 tablespoons milk
1 teaspoon vanilla
1⅓ cups flour
1 teaspoon baking soda
½ teaspoon salt
1 pound of chocolate star candies

Preheat oven to 350 degrees. Mix the shortening and peanut butter together in a large bowl. Add the white sugar and brown sugar and mix. In another bowl, beat the egg with the milk and vanilla. Add to the sugar mixture. In another bowl, mix the flour with the baking soda and salt. Gradually add to the sugar mixture. Form rounded teaspoonfuls of dough into balls. Roll the dough balls in a bit of white sugar and place them on a cookie sheet. Bake for 8 minutes. Take the cookie sheet out of the oven and press a chocolate star into the top of each cookie. Bake for 3 minutes more. Cool on a wire rack.

Christmas Stollen

1 cup golden raisins

1 cup dried cherries

1 cup slivered almonds

⅔ cup orange liqueur

½ cup chopped crystallized ginger

3½ sticks butter, divided

⅓ cup whole milk

4 cups all-purpose flour

1 cup sugar, divided

2¼ teaspoons instant yeast (or one ¼-ounce packet active dry yeast)

2 teaspoons ground ginger, divided

1 teaspoon ground cardamom

1 teaspoon salt

¼ teaspoon ground nutmeg

2 large eggs

1 teaspoon vanilla extract

Oil or butter for greasing the bowl and baking sheet

1½ cups powdered sugar

Combine the raisins, cherries, almonds, orange liqueur, and crystallized ginger in a medium bowl. Stir to combine, cover, and let sit at room temperature while you make the dough or overnight if time allows.

Meanwhile, heat 1 cup (2 sticks) of butter and the milk in a small saucepan over medium-low heat until the butter melts. In a large bowl, combine the flour, ¼ cup of the sugar, yeast, 1 teaspoon of the ground ginger, cardamom, salt, and nutmeg.

When the butter mixture cools, add it to the flour mixture and stir. Lightly beat together the eggs and vanilla and stir them into the dough. Knead the dough until it feels smooth and elastic, about 10 minutes, and set aside. Grease a large bowl (use the same one you mixed the dough in), add the dough, and turn it over to coat it lightly with oil or butter. Cover the bowl with a clean kitchen towel or plastic wrap, put it in a warm place, and let the dough rise until double in size, 1½ to 2 hours.

Punch down the dough and add the raisin mixture. Knead the dough in the bowl until the raisin mixture is evenly mixed in. (The dough will be sticky.) Grease a baking sheet and shape the dough into 2 to 4 long oval loaves on the baking sheet. Cover the baking sheet with a clean kitchen towel, put it in a warm place, and let the loaves rise for 1 hour.

Preheat the oven to 350 degrees. Bake until the loaves are golden brown, about 35 minutes (for smaller loaves) to 1 hour (for larger loaves). When the stollen are done, melt the remaining ¾ cup (1½ sticks) butter in a small saucepan. Brush the tops and sides of the stollen with the butter while the loaves are still warm. Combine the remaining ¾ cup sugar and 1 teaspoon ground ginger and sprinkle over the stollen. Cool thoroughly. Sprinkle the powdered sugar all over the stollen, pressing lightly to help it stick. Wrap each loaf in foil or plastic wrap and let sit at room temperature for at least 1 day before serving.

Ginger Cookies

- 1 cup sugar, plus more for rolling out, if desired
- ¾ cup butter
- ¼ cup molasses
- 1 egg
- 2 cups flour
- 1 teaspoon baking soda
- 1 teaspoon ginger
- ½ teaspoon cinnamon
- ½ teaspoon cloves

Preheat oven to 350 degrees. Beat the sugar, butter, molasses, and egg in a large bowl until creamy. In another bowl, combine the rest of the ingredients and then mix into the sugar mixture. Roll the dough into balls; roll each in a bit of sugar if desired. Place them on a cookie sheet and bake until no imprint remains when you touch a cookie, 8 to 10 minutes.

Christmas Morning Loaf

The directions here are exactly as they appear on the back of Eleanor's recipe card:

1 cup sugar

½ cup shortening

2 teaspoons salt

2 cups milk

¼ cup warm water

2 packages of active dry yeast

2 eggs, beaten

7¾ cups flour

2 cups of mixed candied fruit

1 cup seedless raisins

1½ teaspoons crushed cardamom seed

Mix all together and put in loaves.

Let rise until double in size.

Punch down and put in pans.

Bake about 45 minutes.

CHAPTER 30

BIRTHDAYS

Birthday parties were important for my brothers and me, and I always looked forward to mine with great anticipation. Not only would our mother bake a big birthday cake that day (my favorite was Devil's Food), but in the evening neighbors and relatives would come over for supper. (My brothers, born in

Eleanor made this birthday cake for granddaughter Lisa.

winter, didn't have much of a party, as the relatives came over at noon on the weekend, and of course, as twins, they had to share the occasion.)

There were always candles on the cake, to be blown out while everyone sang "Happy Birthday." And there were presents—not many, because times were tough, but we usually received one special gift. I will never forget my twelfth birthday, the year I turned old enough to buy a hunting license and hunt with my dad. My present was a hunting knife, which I still have. These days, I look at it and recall that birthday celebration and the many years of tramping through the woods and fields with my father.

Another birthday celebration I have never forgotten involved a neighbor girl, Katherine Davis. She never left the farm, staying to take care of her father after her mother died. Her sisters left and married, but Katherine stayed home to work. Alan Davis was not a good farmer (he was a better carpenter); he milked a few cows and raised a few acres of corn, oats, hay, and potatoes, but he scarcely had enough money to put food on the table.

My mother knew the date of Katherine's birthday and one year thought it might be fun to host a little birthday party for her. By now Katherine was in her thirties. Ma made a birthday cake and invited over some of the neighbors. When they all sang "Happy Birthday," Ma noticed that Katherine was crying. "This is the first birthday party I ever had," Katherine said. I have no doubt it was birthday celebration she never forgot. And I never forgot it either.

Devil's Food Cake

¼ cup shortening
1 cup sugar
2 eggs, beaten
½ cup buttermilk
1½ cups flour
½ cup boiling water
2 squares of bitter chocolate
1 teaspoon baking soda
½ teaspoon salt
1 teaspoon vanilla

Preheat oven to 325 degrees. Beat the shortening in a large bowl and add sugar until creamy. Gradually add the beaten eggs and beat hard. Stir in the buttermilk alternately with the flour. In another bowl, pour boiling water over chocolate to melt. Stir quickly and add the baking soda while mixture is still boiling hot. Add the salt. Stir until mixture thickens. Add chocolate mixture to the flour mixture. Add the vanilla and beat hard. Pour batter into a 9 x 13-inch pan and bake until a toothpick inserted into the center comes out clean, about 40 minutes.

Mrs. Sebold's Cream Sponge Cake

This is exactly as it appears on the card. There's no explanation of who Mrs. Sebold was.

4 egg yolks
3 tablespoons cold water
1 teaspoon lemon flavoring
1 cup sugar
1½ teaspoons cornstarch put in cup and fill cup with flour
1¼ teaspoons baking powder
¼ teaspoon salt
4 egg whites

Beat yolks of 4 eggs and water until thick in a bowl. Add lemon flavoring. Add sugar gradually and beat for 2 minutes.

Put cornstarch in a one cup measuring cup and fill with flour. Level off the flour.

Pour the flour and cornstarch into a separate bowl.

Add the baking powder and salt to the flour and stir.

Add the flour mixture to the sugar mixture and mix thoroughly.

Beat the egg whites until stiff.

Add the egg whites to the cake batter and fold in.

Pour the cake batter into a tube pan.

Bake for 30 minutes in a moderate, 375 degrees oven.

Turn pan upside down. Let cool. Remove from pan.

Banana Cake

Eleanor's recipe card has no directions. Watkins sold an "Imitation Maple Flavor" that she probably used.

1½ cups sugar
2 eggs
½ cup shortening
¼ teaspoon salt
¾ teaspoon maple flavoring
7 teaspoons sour milk
3 good sized bananas
2½ cups sifted flour
1 teaspoon baking soda

Bake 50 minutes in moderate oven.

Banana Chiffon Cake

2 cups flour
1½ cups sugar
3 teaspoons baking powder
1 teaspoon salt
7 eggs, separated
¾ cup cold water
½ cup cooking oil
1 medium-sized banana, mashed
1 teaspoon vanilla
½ teaspoon cream of tartar

Preheat oven to 325 degrees. Mix the flour, sugar, baking powder, and salt together in a large bowl. Make a well in the middle of the dry ingredients and pour in the unbeaten egg yolks, cold water, and cooking oil. Mix all ingredients together. Add mashed banana and vanilla and mix well. In a large bowl, beat the 7 egg whites and cream of tartar until very stiff. Fold into other ingredients. Pour the cake batter into an ungreased angel food tube pan. Bake for 55 minutes at 325 degrees; raise oven temperature to 350 degrees and bake for another 10 minutes.

When you take the cake out of the oven, turn it upside down on a cooling rack immediately. Cool for 2 hours. Turn right side up and run a knife around the edge of the pan before removing from the pan. Drizzle cake with your favorite white frosting.

Angel Food Cake

1½ cups powdered sugar
1 cup sifted flour
1½ cups egg whites (You'll need about 12 eggs.)
1½ teaspoons cream of tartar
1½ teaspoons vanilla
⅓ teaspoon salt
½ teaspoon almond extract
1 cup white sugar

Preheat oven to 375 degrees. Mix the powdered sugar and flour together and set aside. In another bowl, combine egg whites, cream of tartar, vanilla, salt, and almond extract and stir briskly until foamy. Gradually add sugar 2 teaspoons at a time and continue mixing. Stir until stiff peaks form into a meringue.

Sprinkle the flour and sugar mixture 3 teaspoons at a time over the meringue. Cut and fold in gently with a spatula, folding down the center and up the side of the bowl. Carefully pour into a 10-inch tube pan. Level off the batter. Pull a knife gently through the batter, widening your circle each time to break up air bubbles. Bake until no imprint remains when you lightly touch your finger to the top of the cake, 30 to 35 minutes. Remove from oven. Turn pan upside down and cool for at least 2 hours. Remove cake from pan.

CHAPTER 31

HOUSEWARMING FOR NEW NEIGHBORS

The news passed quickly around the neighborhood: Andrew Nelson was retiring from farming and had sold his farm. All the neighbors wanted to know who bought the place and when they'd be moving in. Through the neighborhood grapevine, we soon learned their names, Guy and Lena York, and that they had several boys. They were moving to the farm just across the road from what had been Charlie George's place and was now owned by Freddy Rapp.

"Where were the Yorks from?" was a common question. No one seemed to know. Someone opined that they were from the South. I for one was looking forward to getting to know a southern family.

MENU

HOUSEWARMING PARTY

Noodle hotdish	*Chocolate cake*
Pork and beans with ham	*Bar cookies*
Cheese sandwiches	*Beer and coffee*
Dill pickles	

As was the custom in our community, the neighbors organized a housewarming party to be held at the Yorks' farm. Everyone brought something to eat, and everyone showed up, adults and kids of various sizes and ages. My brothers and I played card games with the York boys, Arnold, Jerry, Bob, and Lyle. Dick, the baby, was too young to do anything but watch. The adults visited and got acquainted with Lena and Guy, welcoming them to the neighborhood.

As I played cards with the York boys, I listened to how they talked, hoping to pick up what someone had said would be a southern drawl. I'd never heard a southern drawl, so I didn't know what to listen for. Finally I concluded that the York boys talked just about the same as we did. It was only later that I learned that they had come from someplace in southern Wisconsin, only 150 miles away from Wild Rose.

Noodle Hotdish

Eleanor would have used her own canned vegetables in this hotdish.

- 1 onion, chopped
- 1 tablespoon butter
- 1 pound ground beef
- 1 package (16 ounces) egg noodles, cooked according to directions
- 1 can (30 ounces) whole tomatoes
- 1 can (16 ounces) corn with liquid
- 1 can (16 ounces) peas with liquid
- Crushed potato chips
- ½ cup shredded cheddar cheese

Preheat oven to 350 degrees. Simmer onion in butter in a skillet until it begins to soften. Add the ground beef and simmer until it is browned. Add noodles, tomatoes, and corn and peas with their liquid; stir. Simmer until the ingredients are warmed through. Pour mixture into a casserole dish. Sprinkle some crushed potato chips on top. Bake for 45 minutes. Sprinkle the cheese on top and return to oven until cheese is melted, about 10 minutes.

Filled Oatmeal Bar Cookies

1½ cups chopped dates
1 cup white sugar
1 cup water
1 cup brown sugar
1 cup shortening
2 eggs
2 cups flour
1 teaspoon baking soda
1 teaspoon salt
2½ cups old-fashioned oats

Preheat oven to 350 degrees. Combine dates, white sugar, and water in a saucepan and boil until thick. Remove from heat and cool. In a large bowl, beat together the brown sugar, shortening, and eggs until creamy. Combine the flour, baking soda, and salt and stir into brown sugar mixture. Stir in oats.

Press half of the mixture in a 9 x 13-inch pan. Spread the date filling over the oats mixture. Then cover the dates with the remaining oats mixture. Bake until lightly browned, 30 to 35 minutes. Cool and cut into squares.

CHAPTER 32

GRANDPA WITT'S FUNERAL

My mother's parents, Grandpa and Grandma Witt, lived a little over a mile west of us, where they had been longtime farmers. Grandpa Witt was a good farmer, though unfortunately situated on a rather poor sandy, stony, and hilly farm. He was one of the first in the neighborhood to have electricity generated by a gasoline-powered generator. He also was one of the first farmers in the neighborhood to grow alfalfa.

In early 1941 Grandpa Witt was seventy-four years old and in poor health. His son, Wilbur, and daughter-in-law, Kathryn, lived with Grandma and Grandpa at the time, and Wilbur did most of the farming. Grandpa Witt died on February 11, 1941 (Grandma Witt would die later that year on December 6,

The Witt family at their farm in the 1930s. Grandfather William Witt is on the far left; next to him is Grandmother Amelia Witt.

269

the day before the Pearl Harbor attack). It was common in those days to display the bodies of deceased loved ones in the homes of close relatives. Ma opened up the parlor, usually closed off for the winter, and that is where Grandpa Witt lay in his casket, surrounded by sweet-smelling flowers. Until the day of the funeral, neighbors, relatives, and friends stopped by our farm to share their condolences and to leave a variety of foods.

I was six and a half. Each evening during that time, I passed by the open coffin on my way to bed, sneaking a peak at my dead grandpa and trying to make sense of what was happening. After Grandpa's burial in the church cemetery, under some tall pine trees, friends and relatives were invited to our farmhouse for a lunch. They talked about Grandpa Witt, they laughed, and they ate.

The neighbors brought cakes and casseroles. My mother made sandwiches and provided the pickles. Funerals were sad events, but they also brought friends, relatives, and neighbors together to remember the deceased, to enjoy good food, and to tell stories. Good food made grieving a little easier.

MENU

FUNERAL LUNCH

Ham and pea casserole

Corn and noodle casserole

Bologna sandwiches

Open-faced cheese sandwiches

Homemade white and rye bread with butter

Green Jell-O salad

Homemade pickles: dill, apple, and beet

Assorted cakes and cookies

Coffee

Corn and Noodle Casserole

1 egg
1 cup milk
2 cups cooked egg noodles
1½ cups home-canned corn
1 small onion, chopped
¼ cup soda cracker crumbs
2 tablespoons chopped celery (optional)
Salt, pepper, or paprika, to taste
2 tablespoons melted butter, mixed with some bread crumbs
⅓ cup grated cheese

Preheat oven to 350 degrees and butter a baking dish. Lightly beat egg in a large bowl and then add milk. Add the noodles, corn, onion, cracker crumbs, celery, and seasonings. Mix well. Pour into baking dish. Cover with buttered bread crumbs. Sprinkle the grated cheese on top. Bake 30 minutes.

Green Jell-O Salad

1 package (3 ounces) lime Jell-O
1 cup cottage cheese
¾ cup crushed pineapple
⅓ cup chopped nuts

Grease a Jell-O mold. Prepare Jell-O in a bowl according to package directions. Pour about half of Jell-O mixture into mold. Leave the other half of the Jell-O in the bowl. Refrigerate both until set.

Whip the half in the bowl until foamy. Add the cottage cheese to the foamy Jell-O and stir together. Fold in pineapple and nuts. Pour the cottage cheese mixture on top of the Jell-O in the mold. Refrigerate. Unmold and serve.

CHAPTER 33

4-H CLUB AND BOX SOCIALS

In the fall of 1945, shortly after the end of World War II, Pa said we should organize a 4-H club in our neighborhood. Back in the 1920s, Pa had shown cows at the county fair, and now he thought my brothers and I and the neighbor kids would enjoy the experience as well. The dairy project was a popular one for 4-H members. About half the kids at the Chain O' Lake School were ten years old or older (I was eleven) and thus eligible to join 4-H. Pa drove to Wautoma and met with Henry Haferbecker, the county agricultural agent, to talk about how to organize a club in our school district.

A scene from the Waushara County Fair in Wautoma in the 1950s

A week later, Mr. Haferbecker came out to school one evening and met with all of us ten-and-olders and our parents.

Soon we had formed the Chain O' Lake 4-H club, elected officers, and decided on meeting dates. We chose to meet monthly, each time at a different member's home. At our meetings we talked about our various projects— I had enrolled in the dairy and forestry projects—and afterward we ate a big lunch prepared by the host's mother. The meetings were informative and mostly fun—but the lunches were outstanding. No one ever missed a 4-H meeting, I think in large part because of the great lunches following the meetings.

MENU

4-H MEETING LUNCH

Ground venison sandwiches on buns	*Pickles*
Dressed-up green beans	*Potato chips*
Cranberry supreme salad	*Kool-Aid*

All the members of our 4-H club came from small dairy farms, and each member wanted to take his or her calf to the fair. We all wanted to stay over at the fair to take care of our calves, but where? A dormlike building had been set up for the girls, but there was no place designated for the boys. When I asked about it, Pa said he'd heard that the boys slept with their calves in the cattle barn. I thought that sounded fine, but a few of the parents thought we needed an alternative.

After World War II, surplus army equipment became available at very reasonable prices. Our club decided to buy a surplus army tent, one large enough to sleep six boys plus our 4-H leader, Clayton Owens. There were also surplus army cots available. The tent cost thirty-five dollars, and the cots were five dollars, if I remember correctly. But how could we come up with thirty-five dollars for a tent, when our club treasury had about four bucks in it? We decided to hold two community events: a box social and an ice-cream social. We would advertise them as open to the public, sponsored by the Chain O' Lake 4-H Club as a fundraiser for a used tent for the 4-H boys to sleep in at the county fair.

On a Friday night in late April, our 4-H club hosted our box social at the Chain O' Lake School. We had put up posters at the feed mill, at the Union State Bank, and at the co-op store in Wild Rose announcing the event. And we had asked all of the students at Chain O' Lake School, including those too young for 4-H, to come to the event and bring their parents. On the night of the box social, the schoolroom was filled, almost as full as it was for the annual Christmas program. As I looked around, I saw several people I didn't know—a good sign, as this meant our advertising in Wild Rose had paid off.

At a box social, the women and girls donate a lunch for two, which they prepare and then put in a box that they carefully decorate with tissue paper, ribbons, and whatever other adornments they can find. The boxes are auctioned off to the men in the audience; each winning bidder gets to eat with the woman or girl who prepared the lunch.

The boxes were lined up on desks at the front of the schoolroom. Clayton Owens volunteered to be auctioneer. Soon he was bringing in from two to five dollars for the attractively decorated boxes—most of them were shoeboxes, but a couple were cylindrical Quaker Oats containers. With the auction over, the successful bidders held up their boxes, and the women and girls who had prepared them held up their hands. It was a fun evening, with some people meeting and sharing a lunch with someone they didn't know.

Some of the 4-H members' mothers also brought along food to share, for those who didn't make or buy boxes. We took in about twenty dollars that night, well on our way toward the cost of the used army tent.

MENU

Box Lunch for Two

Cold fried chicken	*Dill pickles*
Cheese sandwiches on homemade white bread	*Molasses cookies*
	Apples

With the success of the box social in mind, we confidently moved ahead to organize our ice cream and pie social. We decided to hold the event on a Saturday night in July at Clayton Owens's farm, which was just a mile or so out of Wild Rose. The residents of the village would surely flock to our ice cream and pie social on a warm summer night.

The 4-H members' mothers made the pies, but our club had to buy the ice cream. We also arranged for a neighbor boy, who had been away but was visiting his parents, to play the accordion during the event.

The crowd was decent, but not outstanding. Whoever was dipping the ice cream was overly generous, and we netted only about ten dollars after paying for the ice cream. It was a fun community event, bringing lots of folks together, but it was far from a money-maker. We were still five dollars short for our tent. Luckily, several of the fathers chipped in, and we eventually had a sturdy tent to sleep in at the county fair.

Ground Venison Sandwiches

1 pound ground venison
½ cup chopped onion
1 can (10½ ounces) tomato soup
½ cup chopped celery
⅓ cup ketchup
1 tablespoon mustard
1 tablespoon Worcestershire sauce
1 teaspoon salt
¼ cup water or enough to make it the consistency that you like
Hamburger buns, for serving

Cook and stir the venison and onion in a skillet until the meat is light brown. Drain. Stir in the remaining ingredients. Cover and simmer over low heat until heated through, 10 to 15 minutes. Serve on hamburger buns.

Dressed-up Green Beans

1 can (14 ounces) green beans
1 beef bouillon cube
⅓ cup onion rings, thinly sliced
4 slices crisp cooked bacon

Drain the can of beans, reserving ¾ cup of the liquid. Combine the liquid with bouillon cube and the onion rings in a large saucepan. Simmer until the onions are soft, about 10 minutes. Add the beans to the saucepan, mix together, and heat through. Crumble the bacon and sprinkle on top of the beans before serving.

Cranberry Supreme Salad

1 package (3 ounces) raspberry Jell-O
2 cups boiling water, divided
1 can (16 ounces) cranberry sauce
1 package (3 ounces) lemon Jell-O
1 small package (3 ounces) cream cheese, softened
⅓ cup mayonnaise
1 can (8½ ounces) crushed pineapple, not drained
1 cup heavy cream, whipped
1 cup small marshmallows

Dissolve raspberry Jell-O in 1 cup boiling water. Add the cranberry sauce. Mix well and let cool. Pour into a 6-cup mold.

Dissolve lemon Jell-O in 1 cup boiling water and let cool. Add cream cheese, mayonnaise, and pineapple with its liquid. Let stand. After the mixture has started to gel, stir in the whipped cream and marshmallows. Pour over the raspberry mixture. Chill overnight.

Fried Chicken

2 to 3 pounds broiler chicken pieces (use breasts, thighs, and legs)
6 tablespoons flour
1 teaspoons salt
1 teaspoon garlic powder
1 teaspoon paprika
1 teaspoon onion salt
⅛ teaspoon pepper
Enough vegetable oil to brown the chicken

Wash chicken pieces and pat dry. Mix together the flour, salt, garlic powder, paprika, onion salt, and pepper. Put the mixture in a paper or plastic bag and add chicken pieces, tossing to coat; or, put the dry mixture on a plate and dredge the chicken.

Fill a heavy skillet with vegetable oil to ½-inch deep and heat until it sizzles when a drop of water is sprinkled in. Add the chicken to the skillet and brown lightly. Don't crowd the chicken in the skillet. (Use two skillets if necessary.) Turn the chicken with tongs and brown on the other side. Browning the chicken will take about 15 to 20 minutes. Reduce the heat and cover tightly. If the oil is being absorbed too quickly, add 1–2 tablespoons of water to the skillet so the chicken doesn't burn. Cook slowly until tender, 30 to 40 minutes. Uncover for last 10 minutes to allow the outer skin to crisp.

OVEN METHOD:
Remove the chicken from the skillets after browning and put in a baking pan. Bake in the oven for 1 hour until tender.

CHAPTER 34

SPECIAL DAYS AT THE COUNTRY SCHOOL

During my growing-up years, our one-room country school, which stood at the intersection of County Highway A and the dirt road that trailed past our farm, was the center of our community. The Chain O' Lake School Board was made up of farmers in the district, and my dad served as its treasurer for many years—even though my mother did most of the check-writing and bookkeeping that was required. People in the district were proud of their school and supportive of the teacher, who often lived with one of the families, including mine, during the school year.

A country school gave the community an identity. When I was asked where I lived, my answer would be "in the Chain O' Lake School District." In the days of my youth, that told people more than "four and a half miles west of Wild Rose." The school was much more than a building where neighborhood kids received eight years of education. It was a gathering place for neighborhood events, and community members, whether they had children at the school or not, attended many of the school's programs; the annual Christmas program was one in particular that nobody missed.

Our teacher, Mrs. Jenks, invited parents to many of our school parties. The first of the year, and one of the most anticipated, was our Halloween party. When I was a kid, no one knew about trick or treating. A few of the older boys in the neighborhood played a few tricks, which mostly meant tipping over outhouses or putting horse harnesses on a neighbor's cows— that sort of thing. But there was no going from house to house hoping for candy. Perhaps it was because the houses were too far apart—at least a half mile. Or maybe it was because the Halloween party at the school was so much fun that walking miles for a little candy made little sense.

Starting in mid-October, we began making cutouts of ghosts and goblins and jack-o-lanterns that we put on the bulletin boards all around the schoolroom. On Halloween, the entire afternoon was set aside for the party. A school board member brought in a big washtub and a bushel of apples, and Mrs. Jenks spent the noon recess hour preparing the room while we kids were instructed to stay outside and not peek.

By one o'clock the mothers began arriving. (Fathers could not get away from farmwork to attend.) A seventh grader carried in water to fill the washtub, into which Mrs. Jenks dumped about twenty of the rosy red apples. One of the mothers tied long strings to the stems of other apples, which were then hung from the ceiling of the entryway. Mrs. Jenks made last-minute adjustments to the guessing game she had organized, which was on her desk in front of the room.

One of the mothers was in charge of the apple-bobbing game. Without using your hands, you tried to retrieve an apple from the washtub. This usually meant you pushed your head all the way to the bottom of the tub so you could bite into the apple, ending up with a very wet head for your effort. Another mother was in charge of the apples hanging from strings. Again using no hands, you tried to bite into one of the apples. If you succeeded, the apple was yours. But the most fun of all was the guessing game. One at a time, students were blindfolded and led to the front of the room, where they were instructed to identify three objects using only their sense of touch. The first bowl contained witches' eyeballs (grapes), the second held witches' fingers (long, slender carrots), and the third contained witches' brains (globs of quilt stuffing). Those who identified the objects correctly received a little bag of Halloween candy. After the activities, everyone enjoyed party treats.

MENU

HALLOWEEN PARTY

Pumpkin bars	*Homemade popcorn balls*
Apple fritter bread	*Orange Kool-Aid*
Assorted cookies	

PIGTAIL SHENANIGANS

In the spirit of using every last morsel of a butchered pig, Pa once found an unusual use for a tail from one of our pigs.

At our annual school Christmas program, held the last Friday before Christmas, Santa Claus made his usual appearance. After a few "ho ho hos" and a couple of "Merry Christmases," he began passing out gifts from the big sack he had slung over his shoulder. After giving gifts to the children and to our teacher, he still had two small presents left. He gave one to my dad and the other to our neighbor Bill Miller.

All eyes turned first to Pa, who began tearing the colorful holiday paper off of a little box. Under the paper, Pa found a matchbox, the kind that held the large kitchen matches that everyone used in those days to light lamps and lanterns. He opened the box, and a very much alive and considerably angry English sparrow flew out. As it circled the schoolroom, everyone clapped and cheered—except for the school board members, who knew it was their responsibility to capture the bird and remove it from the building. The source of the present was unknown, but Pa later learned it had come from Bill Miller.

Bill opened his little package next. It contained the long and hairy pigtail left over from our November hog butchering. Bill smiled and began waving it around, as people cheered and clapped. Although perhaps not quite as creative a gift as a live sparrow in a box, the pigtail had found a second use, long remembered and long talked about.

Our school's annual Christmas program was one of the most important annual events in our community. In addition to enjoying the children's memorized pieces and one-act plays, people had a chance to visit with each other. Following the program, Santa Claus always came by, distributing gifts to the children and to our teacher. Santa also had little bags of hard candy and peanuts in the shell for all the children, including those too young for school. For many years, one community resident who had no children brought Delicious apples, enough so that everyone could go home with a big, bright red apple.

Christmas program at Chain O' Lake School, circa 1954

After Christmas became a distant memory, we began looking forward to our annual Valentine's Day party. In early February, after we had cut out our silhouettes of Presidents Washington and Lincoln, we began making hearts from red construction paper. We hung them up around the schoolroom, which made the place a little more cheery on those long winter days. We also made valentines for our mothers.

From the Sears and Roebuck winter sale catalog, I had ordered inexpensive little valentines, one for each of my twenty or so schoolmates. With our teacher's help, we made a huge box, covered with white paper and plastered with red paper hearts. The box sat on a table in front of the room and into which we stuffed our valentines, carefully selected for each student. For the couple of weeks leading up to the party, we all stared at that colorful box, wondering what fine valentines were inside and which ones had our name on them. By the time I was in eighth grade I discovered that girls weren't just annoying, boring persons, and I wondered what sort of valentine I might get from the cute little seventh grade girl who was very shy but who seemed to be glancing at me every so often.

Mrs. Jenks invited all the mothers to the school for our valentine party, which began at 2 p.m. The mothers all walked to the school, carrying with them valentine cookies and cakes of several kinds. Mrs. Jenks made a big bowl of Kool-Aid.

After everyone had arrived, Mrs. Jenks opened the box and distributed the valentines. Each of us got a valentine from every other student. Many were homemade; others were like the ones I had gotten from the Sears catalog. We also each got a valentine from Mrs. Jenks, and we gave our mothers the valentines we had made for them. From the shy seventh grader, I received a store-bought valentine, a cupid holding a bow and arrow. It contained no message, just the girl's name. She remained a mystery to me.

MENU

Valentine Party

Heart-shaped sugar cookies	*Assorted other cakes*
Aunt Minnie's Googoo Cake	*Cherry Kool-Aid*

The school picnic in May was another highly anticipated event. It signaled the end of the school year, but it also meant a celebration when students, parents, and our teacher all had a chance to eat together, swap stories, and play softball.

The centerpiece of the event was a potluck picnic dinner. Mrs. Jenks sent a notice home with all the students announcing the event and asking people to bring their own eating utensils, sandwiches, and a dish to pass— anything from a casserole to a chocolate cake. The school board bought five gallons of vanilla ice cream that came in two-and-a-half-gallon metal canisters, tucked inside a heavily insulated canvas bag, which kept the ice cream from melting.

The picnic was always held on the last Friday of the school year. A couple members of the school board came by midmorning to set up sawhorses and planks in the schoolyard to make the tables for the food (the same sawhorses and planks they used to make a stage for the Christmas program). Little schoolwork was done that morning, as we all prepared for the picnic, the program, and the softball game to follow. By eleven thirty, parents began arriving, and by noon the makeshift picnic table was groaning with an abundance of good food.

Mrs. Jenks thanked everyone for coming and invited them to eat before the hot food got cold and the cold food got warm. After the meal she said there would be a short program. Families lined up, filled their plates, and found places to sit under the big oak trees that graced the school grounds.

"Don't forget the ice cream," someone on the school board said as we cleaned our plates. This time the children lined up first to get double-scoop ice-cream cones—always a treat, as few of us had electricity and thus could not store ice cream.

When everyone had finished eating, Mrs. Jenks said she had a few words to share. First she thanked the parents for their help during the school year, from helping their children with their homework to assisting with various school events. She thanked the school board members for their support and help. Then she introduced the seventh-graders who had successfully passed the county exams. Everyone clapped when Mildred Swendrznski and Jim Kolka stood up. Finally, she introduced me, the only eighth-grader. She said she was proud of me for passing the day-long county-wide tests held at the Normal School in Wautoma and announced that next year I would be attending high school in Wild Rose.

At last it was time for the softball game. Our school's softball team, along with every other student who wanted to play, took the field. Our opponents would be our fathers. Our team had played softball every school day since the snow melted in late March, while the fathers had not played since last year's picnic. As usual, the school team won. But the best part of the game was the chance to see our fathers play. They were all farmers and seemed to work all the time. For one glorious day in May, they took off a couple of hours to play.

MENU

€ND-OF-SCHOOL-Y€AR PICNIC

Sandwiches brought in by each family	*Assorted cakes, pies, and cookies*
Hotdishes to share	*Pickles*
Strawberry Jell-O	*Lemonade and Kool-Aid*
Rhubarb dessert	

Along with the school-related events, other community celebrations, such as anniversary parties and welcome-home parties, were held at the school. Three of our farmer neighbors, Frank Kolka, Pinky Eserhut, and Harry Banks, often provided music at these gatherings. Frank was Bohemian, Pinky was German (his real name was Alvin), and Harry was an Englishman. One of my first memories of seeing them play together was at an anniversary party the neighborhood held for Bill and Lorraine Miller. The school seats had all been pushed aside, and Frank, with his concertina on his lap, Pinky, with his banjo, and Harry, with his violin, were ready. The threesome played a mix of tunes: old-time polkas, slow waltzes, an occasional schottische, and even played some traditional tunes from Frank's home country, haunting music filled with emotion and meaning.

We were in the grips of the Great Depression, but for one evening, people left their troubles behind. After the dance a huge potluck lunch was served. Everyone went home with a lighter step, feeling for a little while that there may be hope for better days ahead.

When I returned from active duty in the military, the neighbors threw me a welcome-home party at the school. We talked for a while about my time in the army, and then we all enjoyed a potluck lunch. The gathering helped me realize how close the people in the neighborhood were to one another, and how much they cared about what happened to those of us who grew up there. And as always, food was an important part of the celebration.

Pumpkin Bars

4 eggs

2 cups sugar

1 cup cooking oil

1 can (15 ounces) pumpkin (Do not use pumpkin pie filling.)

2 cups flour

2 teaspoons baking powder

2 teaspoons cinnamon

1 teaspoon baking soda

½ teaspoon salt

½ teaspoon ground cloves

½ teaspoon ground ginger

½ teaspoon ground nutmeg

FROSTING

1 small package (3 ounces) cream cheese

6 tablespoons butter

1 tablespoon cream or milk

1 teaspoon vanilla

2–3 cups powdered sugar

Preheat oven to 350 degrees and grease and flour a 12 x 18-inch pan. Mix the eggs, sugar, oil, and pumpkin together in a large bowl. In another bowl, mix together the flour, baking powder, cinnamon, baking soda, salt, cloves, ginger, and nutmeg. Add the flour mixture to the pumpkin mixture. Mix well and pour into pan. Bake 25 to 30 minutes. Let cool before frosting.

To make the frosting, combine cream cheese, butter, cream, and vanilla and beat until smooth. Add powdered sugar and mix until it is a good consistency to spread. Frost the bars.

Apple Fritter Bread

2 apples
⅔ cup plus 2 tablespoons white sugar, divided
2 teaspoons cinnamon, divided
⅓ cup brown sugar
½ cup butter, softened
2 eggs
1½ teaspoons vanilla
1½ cups flour
1¾ teaspoons baking powder
½ cup milk

CRÈME GLAZE
½ cup powdered sugar
1–3 tablespoons cream

Preheat oven to 350 degrees and grease a loaf pan. Peel and chop the apples. Mix with 2 tablespoons white sugar and 1 teaspoon cinnamon. Set aside.

Mix the brown sugar and remaining 1 teaspoon cinnamon in a bowl and set aside. In another bowl, cream the remaining ⅔ cup white sugar and butter until smooth. Beat in the eggs one at a time, and then add the vanilla. In another bowl, combine the flour and baking powder. Add to the creamed butter and sugar mixture and stir until blended. Mix the milk into the batter until smooth.

Pour half of the batter into loaf pan. Sprinkle half of the apple-sugar mixture onto the batter in the pan. Lightly pat the apples into the batter. Pour the remaining batter over the apple layer. Top with the remaining apple mixture. Lightly pat the apples into the top layer of batter. Sprinkle with reserved brown sugar and cinnamon mixture. Bake until a toothpick inserted into the center comes out clean, 50 to 60 minutes. Let cool.

To make the Crème Glaze, stir the powdered sugar and cream together until well mixed. Drizzle over cooled Apple Fritter Bread.

Homemade Popcorn Balls

5 cups popped popcorn
1 cup dry-roasted peanuts
½ cup sugar
½ cup corn syrup
½ cup peanut butter
½ teaspoon vanilla

Combine the popcorn and peanuts in a large bowl and set aside. In a large saucepan over medium heat slowly pour the sugar into the corn syrup. Bring the mixture to a rolling boil while stirring. Remove from the heat. Carefully stir the peanut butter and vanilla into the corn syrup mixture. When the peanut butter has just melted, quickly pour the mixture over the popcorn and peanut mixture. Stir to coat the popcorn well. Let cool. When you can handle the popcorn, shape it into balls. Let rest until completely cool. Wrap each ball in wax paper or plastic wrap.

Aunt Minnie's Googoo Cake

3 cups cake flour, sifted before measuring
2 cups sugar
3 teaspoons baking powder
1 teaspoon salt
½ cup butter
1½ cups milk
1 teaspoon lemon flavoring
4 egg whites, beaten until stiff

Preheat oven to 350 degrees and lightly grease the bottom of a 9 x 13-inch cake pan. Mix together the cake flour, sugar, baking powder, and salt in a large bowl. Cut the butter into the dry ingredients using two forks or a pastry cutter until crumbly. Add the milk gradually, stirring after each addition, until milk is incorporated and batter is thoroughly mixed and smooth. Fold in the lemon flavoring. Gently fold in beaten egg whites. Pour cake batter into the pan and bake for 40 minutes. Let cool. Cake can be dusted with powdered sugar or lightly frosted. Can also use as base for a fresh fruit topping.

Chocolate Chip Cookies

1 cup butter
¾ cup brown sugar
¾ cup white sugar
2 eggs, beaten
1 teaspoon vanilla
2¼ cups flour
1 teaspoon salt
1 teaspoon baking soda
1 teaspoon hot water
1 cup chocolate chips
½ cup chopped nuts

Preheat oven to 350 degrees. Beat the butter and sugars until smooth. Add the eggs and vanilla and stir until smooth. In another bowl, mix the flour and salt. Combine the baking soda with hot water. Mix the flour with baking soda mixture into the sugar mixture until it is mixed in thoroughly. Stir in the chocolate chips and nuts. Make little cookie balls and bake on cookie sheets until golden brown, 8 to 10 minutes.

Strawberry Jell-O Salad

1 large package (6 ounces) strawberry Jell-O

¾ cup boiling water

1 can (13 ounces) crushed pineapple, drained

2½ cups sliced strawberries, washed and cut up (or one 20-ounce package of frozen whole strawberries)

3 bananas, sliced or mashed

1 pint sour cream

Dissolve Jell-O in boiling water in a large bowl and cool. Add pineapple, strawberries, and bananas. Pour half of mixture into a mold and refrigerate about 1 hour. Spread sour cream in a layer over Jell-O. Pour remaining Jell-O over the top of the sour cream and refrigerate until it sets.

Rhubarb Dessert

½ cup butter
2 cups sugar, divided
1 cup buttermilk
1 egg
1 teaspoon vanilla
2 cups flour
1 teaspoon baking soda
2 teaspoons cinnamon, divided
½ teaspoon salt
2 cups cut-up rhubarb
½ cup chopped nuts

Preheat oven to 350 degrees and grease a 9 x 13-inch pan. Beat the butter and 1½ cups of the sugar in a large bowl until creamy. Add the buttermilk, egg, and vanilla and mix well. In another bowl, mix the flour, baking soda, 1 teaspoon cinnamon, and salt. Add to the sugar mixture. Fold in the rhubarb. Pour into pan. To make the topping, combine the remaining ½ cup sugar, remaining teaspoon cinnamon, and chopped nuts. Sprinkle on the batter. Bake for 45 minutes.

Potato Chip Cookies

1 cup butter
1 cup sugar
1 egg
1 teaspoon vanilla
2 cups flour
½ teaspoon baking soda
1 cup crushed potato chips
1 cup butterscotch chips (optional)

Preheat oven to 350 degrees. Beat the butter and sugar together in a large bowl until creamy. Add the egg and vanilla and mix well. Stir in the flour and baking soda and blend well. Stir in the crushed potato chips. Stir in butterscotch chips, if desired. Roll dough into balls, place on a cookie sheet, and press with a fork. Bake until lightly browned, 8 to 10 minutes.

CHAPTER 35

FOOD FOR THOUGHT

When I was growing up, food was central to our lives. If we weren't growing and preparing food for our table, we were growing feed for our livestock. In many ways, my family was blessed. I don't remember ever going to sleep hungry, even during the Depression years; that was not the case for some of our neighbors who did not have enough food.

From a young age I understood that eating was much more than simply consuming food in order to live. My earliest memories are of my father and mother and my twin brothers and me sitting down at our kitchen table for breakfast, dinner, and supper. It was around our old, well-worn wooden kitchen table where we shared what we were doing in school, where Pa told us about the work he had lined up for us in the coming days, and where Ma reported on how well the chickens were doing. We weren't allowed to leave the table until everyone had finished eating, and we ate what was put on our plates, no matter if we thought we wouldn't like it (for me this meant I would eat Ma's homemade rhubarb sauce, which I hated; my brother Don had to face many a plate of loathsome peas).

Pa did not believe in eating in restaurants, unless you were out of town, and even then he usually stopped at a butcher shop and bought a ring of bologna and some saltine crackers for lunch. As a family, we never once ate in a restaurant in the sixteen years I lived at home. Pa would say, "We've got plenty to eat at home, why would we want to eat at a restaurant?" I believe he thought restaurant eating was for city people—country folk did things differently, especially when it came to food and eating. I ate my first restaurant meal when I was about ten years old and Ross Caves, our livestock trucker from Wild Rose, asked if I'd like to ride along with him in his cattle truck to the Milwaukee stockyards where he was delivering a load of hogs that Pa was selling. He often asked farm kids to accompany him to Milwaukee, to keep him company on the long trip and to show the kids a little of the big city.

We arrived in Milwaukee about noon, and after he had unloaded the hogs, Ross asked me if I was hungry. Of course I was. We headed for a little restaurant at the edge of the stockyards, found a table, and Ross said I could order anything I wanted—he was buying. It was the first time I had ever been in a restaurant, and the first time I'd seen a restaurant menu. I couldn't believe all the choices. After a bit, Ross asked me if I'd figured out what I wanted. I said I guess I'd just like some meat and potatoes, a piece of bread, and a glass of milk.

Ross smiled, and when the waitress came to take our orders, Ross told her what I wanted. When my meal arrived, I saw three huge slabs of roast beef, a mound of mashed potatoes with brown gravy, a little pile of carrots and peas, and two slim slices of bread. I dug in. The beef was tender, the mashed potatoes close to what Ma prepared, the glass of milk cold, the carrots and peas passable, but the bread had no taste at all. Finally I understood how much Ma's homemade bread out-shone the commercially prepared kind. It was my first time comparing things I ate in a restaurant to my mother's home cooking—something I have done in one way or another ever since.

By the time I was thirteen or fourteen and old enough to drive a team on a threshing crew, I was introduced to many new foods as the threshing machine moved from farm to farm in our neigh-borhood. At the time I didn't appreciate how diverse our community was in terms

The Apps family, circa 1946. Back row: Eleanor and Herman. Front row: Darrel, Jerold, and Donald.

of ethnic backgrounds: the Kolkas were Czechoslovakian, the Millers and Handrichs were German, the Alan and Griff Davis families were Welsh, the Nelsons were Norwegian, the Macijeskis and the Mushinskis were Polish, the Stuckolas were Russian, and the Jenks and DeWitt families were English. When we ate threshing or corn-shredding or wood-sawing meals at these farms, we always got a sampling of ethnic foods along with the standard meat-and-potatoes fare.

Food was always present at times of happiness in our community— weddings, anniversaries, and neighborhood dances. But it was also a way of helping a family cope in challenging times or grieve when they lost a loved one. When folks learned that my mother would be in the hospital in Fond du Lac for a week or longer after a goiter operation, everyone in the neighborhood brought food, along with offering to help in any way they could.

Food, essential for living, also contributed toward making a life. Its importance went well beyond mere sustenance to our rural community.

INDEX

Note: Recipes appear in **bold** type. Page numbers in *italics* refer to images.

JERRY APPS has been a rural historian and environmental writer for more than forty years. He is a former county extension agent and professor for the University of Wisconsin College of Agricultural and Life Sciences. He is the author of many books on rural history, country living, and environmental issues, including *Old Farm: A History* and *Garden Wisdom: Lessons Learned from 60 Years of Gardening*. Jerry and his wife, Ruth, divide their time between their home in Madison and their farm, Roshara, in Waushara County.

SUSAN APPS-BODILLY has been an elementary and middle school teacher for more than twenty years. She is the author of *One Room Schools: Stories from the Days of 1 Room, 1 Teacher, 8 Grades*. Susan lives in Madison with her husband, Paul. When she's not reading, teaching, or writing, she loves biking or hiking in the woods with her family.